COMPLIMENTS OF

IVY FUNDS®
THE WORLD COVERED℠

Amy Florian

NO LONGER AWKWARD

Communicating with Clients Through the
Toughest Times of Life

Amy Florian

Copyright © 2013 by Corgenius, Inc.

All Rights Reserved

Contributions by Ken Florian
Designed by Tanya Johnston

ISBN 978-0615544458
Library of Congress Control Number: 2013930262

Corgenius, Inc.
815 Woodlawn Street
Hoffman Estates, IL 60169

Ordering Information:
Quantity sales. Special discounts are available on quantity purchases by corporations,
associations, U.S. trade bookstores and wholesalers, and others.
For details, contact the publisher at the address above.

www.Corgenius.com
Printed in the United States of America

First Edition

Dedication

John Willenborg was an earthy Iowa farm boy whose easy laugh and generosity of heart endeared him to everyone he met. Life was simple for John. It was defined by love—for people, animals, God, the land, and most especially for me, whom he loved with his entire being. That love deepened as we lived through two difficult miscarriages, and it burst with joy when our long-awaited baby boy was born.

A mere seven months later, tragedy swept the joy out of my life. John was killed in a car accident, leaving me a twenty-five-year-old widow with an infant son. Unfathomable grief overwhelmed my soul, yet I knew I had to heal: Carl no longer had a father, so he'd better have a mother. Tossed by unpredictable waves of emotion, needing to redefine my purpose, identity, dreams, and very existence, I grasped for whatever resources I could find. Ever so slowly, I began to grow, heal, and gain wisdom forged in the crucible of pain. In the process, I found myself instinctually reaching out to others in grief, teaching them what I knew while continually learning more from them. John's love and his death reshaped the boundaries of my life and set me on a path I never could have anticipated.

Several years later, I met Ken Florian, a highly intelligent, extremely well-read, deeply curious, and selflessly giving man with a profound compassion for those who suffer. Our journeys were not the same, yet threads of our experiences intertwined, informing and broadening the tapestry. Grappling with the implications of John's life and death for our relationship as a couple further defined and informed my perspective. In the meantime, Carl bonded with Ken and in fact began to call him "Dad" as soon as we announced our engagement.

I began doing more work in bereavement, teaching sessions and helping to found a support group for widowed people. Ken encouraged me to return to graduate school to combine my expanding body of on-the-ground knowledge with research and the insights of psychology and thanatology. He proudly framed my master's diploma and my first paycheck for an article. He cheered when I was hired to teach graduate classes. He challenged me when my reasoning was weak, shared information from his own reading, and promoted my personal and professional growth.

It was Ken's inspiration to bring grief education to professionals: although they do not have ready access to this knowledge, their success is strongly influenced (or is dependent upon) it. Under his guidance, we formed Corgenius. In this gratifying work, we help people both personally and professionally. We constantly receive e-mails, phone calls, letters, and texts thanking us for making a distinct difference in people's personal and professional lives.

Without John and without Ken, I would not be here, and this book would not be in your hands. To the men who have so lavishly loved and supported me, I dedicate this book. May it bring you knowledge, competence, skill, and healing.

Amy Florian

Table of Contents

Dedication 7

Table of Contents 9

Preface 13
    Information You Need to Succeed 13
    Easy to Navigate 13
    Learning More 14
    Kindly Give Us Feedback 14

About the Author 15

Background Information 17
    The Nature of Grief 17
    Grief Triggers 18
    Styles of Grieving 19
    Disenfranchised Grief 20
    Ambiguous Loss 21
    Anticipatory Grief 22

What *Not* to Say: Things That Alienate or That Simply Aren't Helpful 25
    Fourteen Things *Not* to Say 25

What *to* Say: Twenty-Two Options That Comfort 31

Eight-Step Protocol for Services After a Death 39
    Delivering a Life Insurance Benefits Check 42

When a Grieving Client Comes into the Office 47
    Setting the Appointment 47
    Offering a Portfolio Notebook 48
    Helpful Set-Up Tips 48

Invite the Story 49

Questions to Ask during Positive Transitions 51

Tears and Tissues 52

Addressing Fears 53

Putting Off Major Decisions 54

Checking in on Your Level of Support 55

End with Normalization and Assurance 55

Emotional Differences Between Divorce and Widowhood 57

Special Issues 61

Clients needing professional help 61

When the Loss Involves Young Children 62

Suicide 64

Murder or Violent Death 66

Documents Every Client Should Have 69

Background Information 69

The Most Important Documents 70

To Remember or Not To Remember: Is It Dementia? 79

Forgetful Clients 79

Clients with Dementia 79

Your Office Protocol for Dementia 81

Clients with Terminal Illness 85

Background Information 85

Durable Powers 85

Watch for Fatigue 86

Concrete Help 86

Four Things That Matter Most 87

Hospice 88

A Necessary Agenda 89

The Possibility of a Family Meeting 89

Statistics and Stories to Demonstrate Knowledge and Raise the Topic of Planning 95

A Few Principles to Incorporate 95

Statistics That Reinforce the Topic 96

Stories that reinforce the topic 97

Value of Role-Play 100

Compensation 101

When Your Pen Hovers Over the Page: Condolence Cards and When to Send Them 103
    General Information and Schedule 103
    Texts of cards 104
    Longer Texts: Letters for Various Intervals 117

Articles for Clients 125
    A Positive Decision on Love..125
    Anything and Everything, Except the Obvious 129
    Chasing After Closure 130
    The Starting Point—Filling the Emptiness 131
    Grieve with Hope 132
    How to Handle Your Fears After the Death of a Spouse 133
    Keeping Busy 136
    Naming the Big White Elephant 137
    The Changing Palette 138
    The Fog of Grief: A Widow's Essay 139
    The Greatest Gift..140
    Twelve Steps for Healthy Grieving 142

Where Do I Turn? Recommended Books on Grief and Loss 145
    Before a Death Occurs..146
    General Grief...146
    Death of a Spouse...149
    Parental Death – for Adults 151
    Child Death – for Parents or Siblings 153
    Books For and About Children or Teens..155
    Divorce..157
    Dementia 159
    Death by Suicide 160
    Murder or Violence..162
    Pet Death 162

Conclusion...165
    Keep In Touch 165

Bibliography of Resources Used...167

Preface

Information You Need to Succeed

You constantly encounter grieving clients. Their grief may be triggered by a death in the family, divorce, job loss, empty nest, retirement, dementia, a serious or terminal diagnosis, market collapse, or any other major life transition.

At these times, do you stumble over timeworn phrases and unintentionally alienate clients who are already in pain? If so, you will lose them. On the other hand, when you effectively walk clients through the toughest times of their lives, you have them for life. Moreover, you gain the trust of their family, friends, and associates.

Yet training programs that address grief and transition are rare. Even when workshops exist, they often reflect the experience of a particular financial or service professional rather than the deep knowledge of an expert in thanatology (the field of death and grief). Therefore, most professionals rely on what they've picked up from others along the way, inadvertently perpetuating mistakes that hurt their business. You need fresh knowledge from an expert,

keen insights that expand your perspective, and practical applications that have a profound impact on client relationships.

That is why *No Longer Awkward* exists. Here, you receive training you can't get anywhere else. These skills, grounded in solid research, equip you to distinguish yourself in the field, serve your clientele in ways others don't, and build your business with engaged clients who enthusiastically refer you to others.

Easy to Navigate

Every chapter in this reference guide is concise and to the point, with only a few pertinent examples and little of the extensive background research that undergirds the skills. It is perfect for when you need answers fast.

Educational information you can use is first on the agenda. When you need to communicate with clients, go to later chapters for condolence card texts, letters, articles, and books to recommend or give.

Learning More

If you wish to deepen your training, we invite you to register for our multi-day class with Corgenius. There, we hone your skills with role-play, written exercises, and group discussion so you thoroughly assimilate the knowledge and are prepared to train others in your office. You also gain a nationwide network of other attendees and graduates, so you can share best practices and raise the bar even higher.

We are committed to giving you what you need to support your grieving clients and differentiate yourself in the marketplace. It is good for your clients, who benefit from the genuine and effective support you offer. It is good for you, increasing the satisfaction and meaning you derive from your work. Finally, it is good for business because you build trust, long-term engagement, and ready referrals.

Kindly Give Us Feedback

As you learn and apply these skills, please give us your stories and your feedback. We will regularly update and revise this guide, further tailoring it to the needs of our readers.

Don't hesitate to contact us with questions or any additional needs you have. E-mail us at hello@corgenius.com or call us at 847-882-3491. We are here to help you succeed.

Remember: Clients look for more than good products and services. They look for professionals who understand their lives, so they can give them their business.

About the Author

The most formative experience in Amy Florian's life occurred when her husband died in a car accident at the age of twenty-five, leaving her a widow with a seven-month-old son. She subsequently dedicated herself to teaching about transition, death, and grief, so others could learn how to effectively companion people through the toughest times of life.

Amy holds a master's degree and is a Fellow in Thanatology (the highest level of certification through the Association for Death Education and Counseling, achieved by fewer than 200 people in the United States). Amy worked with more than 2,000 grieving people over the past twenty-five years. She teaches graduate and undergraduate courses at universities in the Chicago area and facilitates an ongoing support group for widowed persons that she helped found in 1988. She has published more than ninety articles and has international recognition as a unique, inspirational, and powerful presenter at conferences, in-office training, and client seminars. The depth of her knowledge and experience is exceeded only by her passion, which shows through in everything she does.

Contact Corgenius for more information about hiring Amy to teach sessions at your office or upcoming event.

Background Information

The Nature of Grief

We rightly associate grief with death because it is such a well-known trigger. Surviving the death of a loved one serves as the most frequent example used in this guidebook. Yet it is vitally important to recognize that grief is an adaptive response to loss of any kind. Grief occurs whenever an attachment is broken—whenever you must leave behind someone, something, a function, a way of life, or anything else you've become attached to and do not want to live without. It occurs whenever one chapter is ending and another begins and encompasses the "in-between" space when you learn to let go of what can no longer be, accommodate your life to that loss, and build a different future. Grief is the hallway between the room one must leave and the room that awaits.

Grief is neither an illness nor a pathological condition. It is an expected and normal process that allows you to maintain connections to what you lost while you simultaneously assimilate, accommodate, and go forward with life. Grief helps you make sense of the past, create a memory out of what can no longer be, and incorporate the memory into a new, hope-filled future.

The grief process is wrought with pain, paradox, and tension—things we all prefer to avoid. Yet suppressing, denying, or ignoring grief will not make it go away. It festers within and, like a volcano's molten lava, it pushes its way through to the surface. When people deny or ignore

Six types of Loss

Material
Relationship
Intra-psychic
Functional
Role-loss
Routines

grief, they can experience physical effects like headaches, backaches, and stomachaches. Grief finds emotional outlets, especially anger, impatience, and disproportionate reactions. Repressed grief can manifest as clinical depression. Tragically, unresolved grief can cripple a person who never fully lives again because there is too much hidden hurt, risk, and fear.

On the other hand, those who engage the grief process can emerge from the experience better, happier, and healthier, more tolerant of others, wiser, and more appreciative of life and all it holds. No teacher is as adept as the grief process if we are willing to learn.

Grief Triggers

Because loss is ubiquitous throughout the life cycle, you face grieving clients more frequently than you think. Herbert Anderson and Kenneth Mitchell (in the book *All Our Losses, All Our Griefs*) listed six types of loss or transition that trigger grief. They noted that most transitions involve more than one of these intertwining losses. Each individual loss may be sudden (natural disaster) or gradual (Lou Gehrig's disease), total (divorce) or partial (distancing of a once cherished friendship), and temporary (wearing a cast for six weeks) or permanent (amputation).

The six types of grief-triggering loss are as follows:

1. **Material: loss of a physical object, personal and/or sentimental possession, or familiar surroundings**
   » *A treasured possession is broken, lost, or stolen*
   » *A home burns down or is damaged/destroyed by a force of nature*
   » *A car is totaled*
   » *Money is lost in a market collapse, fraud, failed business venture, or gambling spree*
   » *A family moves to a new home and leaves the old one behind*
   » *Elderly people move into an assisted living community*

2. **Relationship: partial or complete loss of a human or animal relationship**
   » *Death of a family member, friend, or business colleague*
   » *Divorce or separation*
   » *Dissolution of a business partnership*
   » *Cooling or distancing of a valued friendship*
   » *Death of a pet*
   » *Betrayal or infidelity*

3. **Intrapsychic: loss of a dream, whether the focus of the dream is oneself or others**
   » *Infertility*
   » *Marriage breakup*
   » *Parenting a child with disabilities whose age-mates begin doing things he or she will never do*
   » *Unfulfilled goals for life, career, or avocation*
   » *Loss of plans and hopes for a future with a person who dies*
   » *A failed business venture or entrepreneurship*

4. **Functional: temporary or permanent loss of a physical, cognitive, or mental capability**
   » *Losses associated with aging: arthritis, eyesight, hearing, energy levels, or ability to do the things one used to do*
   » *Partial or total paralysis of parts of the body*
   » *Dementia*
   » *Loss of driving privileges*
   » *Injury or illness that affects mental capacity*
   » *Joint replacement that places permanent limits on some functions*
   » *Temporary loss of ability following surgery, accidents, etc.*

5. **Role: loss of one's customary identity or "place" in a family structure, work organization, faith center, or other setting**
   » *A promotion to or a demotion from a position*
   » *An adult child must care for a formerly independent parent*

≫ *Parents become empty nesters, or empty nesters take in their grown child*
≫ *A stay-at-home parent goes to work or vice versa*
≫ *A student graduates and moves into the full-time workforce or vice versa*
≫ *A natural caregiver becomes a care receiver*
≫ *A pastor is assigned to a different congregation*
≫ *A breadwinner can no longer hold a job*
≫ *A business owner sells the business to another person or entity*

6. **Routines: loss of the familiar structure of one's life**
   ≫ *Retiring*
   ≫ *Taking on a job that involves a very different amount of travel*
   ≫ *Becoming a parent with all the interruptions to sleep, activities, and freedom*
   ≫ *Adjusting to regular visits to the hospital, nursing home, or other locations*
   ≫ *Entering a rehab facility*
   ≫ *Moving to a nursing home or other facility with scheduled meals and activities*
   ≫ *Enrolling in evening or weekend classes in addition to one's job*
   ≫ *Adjusting to changes when the "social calendar" spouse is absent through divorce, death, or dementia.*
   ≫ *Renegotiating responsibilities in a marriage or partnership*

Note that even positive transitions (retiring, getting married, having a baby) trigger grief. In fact, three of the top ten stress-inducing life events on the widely accepted Holmes-Rahe scale are positive transitions. Although they desire and eagerly anticipate the change, clients must leave a great deal behind and move toward an unfamiliar future.

Note that a client's grief will be deeper and more persistent when there are multiple triggers. During divorce, for instance, every grief trigger is involved except functional loss. When a family member has a severe illness requiring hospitalization and/or long-term care, all of the grief triggers may be involved. Therefore, do your best to be aware of the factors at work for each transition your clients face, so you can name their experience and support them through it.

The principles of grief support discussed in this reference guide apply to all six types of losses. With variations to allow for the nature and depth of the loss, you can ask the same type of questions of a bereaved parent that you'd ask a client whose father has dementia. You demonstrate compassion to a client whose house burned down with the same principles that guide your response to a client whose business failed.

Learn and practice effective grief support skills to make a positive difference through the many and varied transitions in your clients' lives.

Styles of Grieving

Common wisdom suggests that men grieve differently than women. That is not necessarily true. Grief correlates more to style than to gender. In fact, if you prejudge how clients will grieve based on their gender, you risk alienating them.

Intuitive Instrumental

The following two styles of grieving were developed through the research of prominent psychologists Kenneth Doka and Terry Martin and reported in their book *Grieving Beyond Gender: Understanding the Ways Men and Women Mourn.*

a. Intuitive grievers
   Intuitives experience grief as a deep feeling that they must express and talk through. They process and tell their story repeatedly. They are more likely to keep a journal. They seek out support groups and other people in

similar situations. The types of questions they are most likely to ask include the following:

- "Who can emotionally understand and advise me?"
- "Who can I talk to about my feelings?"
- "What books can I read so I know I am not alone?"

b. Instrumental grievers

Instrumentals experience grief in physical, cognitive, or behavioral ways. They want to face facts and take actions. They try to remain objective and analyze the experience. They are more likely to go it alone than to seek support groups and are wary of emotions that might cloud their judgment. They are most likely to ask questions like the following:

- "What concrete actions do I need to take to get through this?"
- "How can I manage my grief and move on?"
- "How can I keep my emotions in check so they don't hold me back?"

It is statistically true and probably consonant with your experience that more women lean to the intuitive side of the spectrum, while more men are instrumentals. Nevertheless, make no assumptions. Some women are strongly instrumental, and some men fall squarely in the intuitive camp. In addition, the distribution of grieving styles falls along a continuum. Few people are entirely one or the other; most function as a blend of both. Adding to the complexity, many people function as intuitive grievers with some losses but grieve instrumentally with others, or professionals who naturally lean to the intuitive side may feel pressure to function in the office as instrumentals.

Therefore, you risk being totally off base if you determine how your clients will grieve based on their gender. Instead, accommodate both styles without judgment.

Think about your own experience and try to determine where you land on the spectrum. Use that awareness along with information in this book to recognize and develop fluency in both styles so you can effectively companion all of your clients, even those who grieve differently than you.

Disenfranchised Grief

Not every loss receives adequate validation in our society, largely because we value particular types of relationships more than others. Perhaps, for instance, you have clients who report that when a beloved pet died, people "consoled" them by saying "At least it was only a cat."

When society at-large doesn't value a relationship, we grant less credence to the loss experience, deny the possibility of deep grief, and may exclude the griever from even rudimentary support. Employment policies sometimes codify the disenfranchisement: for instance, when they allow bereavement leave for the death of an immediate family member but not for the death of a lifelong best friend or a cousin who is emotionally closer than a sibling. Instead of receiving the support and empathy they need, bereaved clients in these situations feel isolated and misunderstood. "Disenfranchised grief" is the psychological term first used by Kenneth Doka in 1989 for losses that we poorly support or understand.

Examples of disenfranchised losses include the following:

≫ *Death of an ex-spouse*
≫ *Death or disability of a partner in a committed same-sex relationship*
≫ *Death of a pet*
≫ *Miscarriage or stillbirth*
≫ *Infertility*

- *Death of an adult sibling (grief support services concentrate on parents and children of the deceased rather than the brothers and sisters)*
- *Death of an elderly or infirm family member*
- *Material loss by fire or natural disaster (the "we-still-have-each-other" syndrome, in which gratitude for people negates legitimate sorrow over the loss of home or treasured possessions)*
- *Loss of an online friend or long-term gaming companion*
- *Death of the person to whom a loved one donated organs*
- *Children or others who are not allowed to attend services or who are not supported in their bereavement*

The list goes on. Your task is to take every client grief seriously, including those that seem trivial to you. Always ask clients what it's like for them and listen with compassion, acknowledging any disenfranchisement. Every time you notice and understand a client's experience when others don't, you distinguish yourself and reinforce a relationship that will last.

Ambiguous Loss

"Ambiguous loss", a term first coined by psychologist Pauline Boss, refers to incomplete, ongoing loss with no definitive closure, or loss that is impossible to resolve.

Most ambiguous losses fall into two categories:

1. A person is physically absent but psychologically present: for example, a soldier missing in action, a kidnapped child who can't be found, or a family member who either abandoned the family or ran away. Ambiguous loss is also a factor when a loved one is declared dead but the body cannot be recovered, leaving family members with questions about whether a death has occurred.

Clients in these situations maintain hope that their loved ones will return, although over time that hope becomes increasingly tenuous. Eventually, as the practical implications of the person's absence press in, the family is forced to adjust to life as if the person died. In the midst of uncertainty over their loved one's fate, they live with constant tension over how much to let go versus how much to cling to hope for return. This deeply stressful, long-term process is often poorly supported.

2. A person is physically present but psychologically absent: for example, a family member who lives in the home but is emotionally distant, a loved one in a persistent vegetative state, or a loved one living with dementia, significant brain trauma, or severe disability.

In these cases, the physical body is still there and alive, needing care, and usually dependent on the family. At the same time, your clients mourn the inch-by-inch loss of the person who once inhabited the body. Their loved one may be growing gradually more distant or seem to have already gone from them. This is particularly the case if the person is in an unrecoverable coma or if he or she has reached the point of no longer recognizing familiar people and remembering their visits.

Since the loved one is present in body only, clients may anguish over decisions about how often to visit or what it means when they do. They may be facing significant medical costs, anguish over treatment decisions, and struggles with adjusting to life in light of the ambiguity. Be prepared to support your client through the complexities of this difficult and painful situation.

Anticipatory Grief

When an unexpected or sudden loss occurs, survivors are thrown into the crucible as their lives are immediately and unalterably changed. Sometimes, though, a loss comes slowly over time, as when a person slides gradually but inexorably toward his or her final breath. Grief does not wait for the actual event. People also grieve in anticipation of a loss they know is coming.

Examples:

a. As high school seniors prepare to move out of the house or go away to college, their parents, already grappling with the childhood that is no more, anticipate their child's absence and the loss of a relationship quality that is only possible when people live together. Parental grief is often deeper than that of their children, since parents anticipate diminishment of their home lives, while children anticipate the excitement and adventure of widening their world.

b. When clients decide to downsize their home, the entire family has to leave behind memories that sing from every wall and activities that occurred in every room. They grieve the impending loss of place since someone else will move in and this will never be "home" to them again. They may find themselves frequently sitting in favorite places, taking in cherished views, remembering and grieving. Even when the move makes logical sense, it is fraught with emotion.

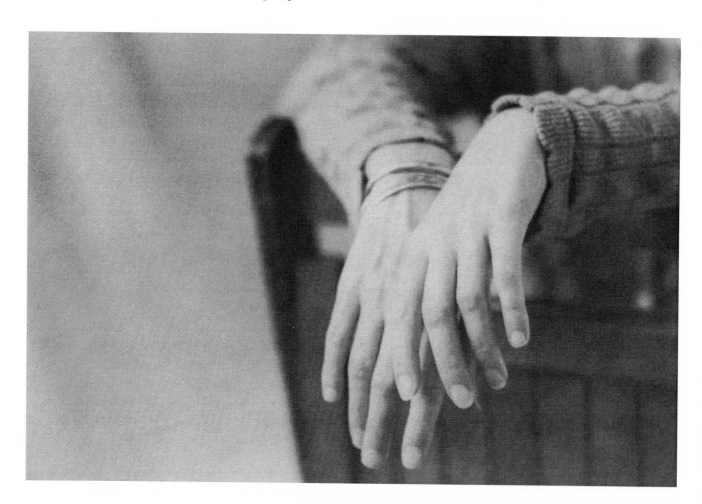

c. As parents age—and especially when they encounter increasing health problems—both they and their children begin to anticipate inevitable outcomes and become more concretely aware of death. They mourn each time a function, ability, or aspect of physical appearance slips away, each additional medical issue, and each bit of evidence that the parents are gradually and inexorably approaching death.

It takes awareness and courage for family members to resist the urge to protect against pain by detaching too soon, but everyone benefits if they can stay engaged and continue to share their joys and sadness with each other.

In all cases of anticipatory grief, name the reality for your clients. Let them know it is normal to grieve both present and impending losses. Invite their stories, and listen as they share their experience with you, especially as it changes over time. Be there for them in ways that others aren't.

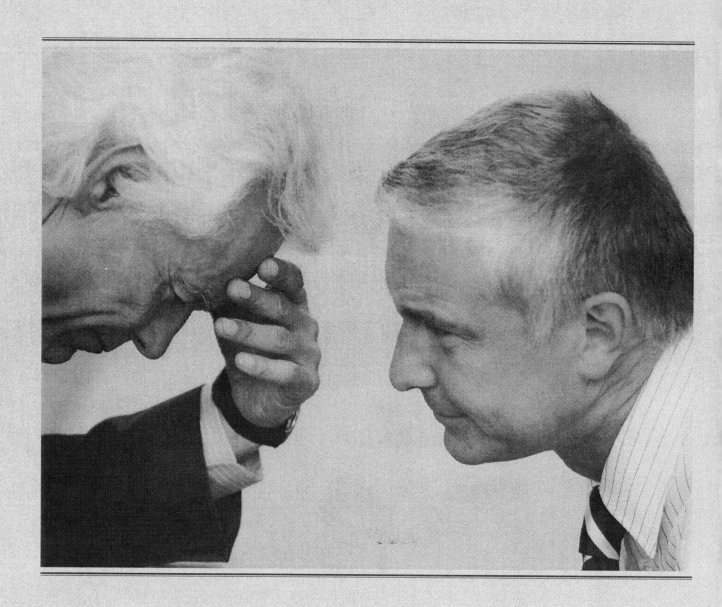

What *not* to Say:
Things That Alienate or That Simply Aren't Helpful

Because we are never taught what to say when someone is grieving, we pick up what we can by listening to others. Unfortunately, that just perpetuates mistakes. To break the cycle, avoid the following list. Some are general caveats. Others apply to specific situations.

You will no doubt be surprised that some of these are unwise; you've heard and said them for years. Yet, when you employ these phrases, your impact will be neutral at best. At worst, you risk unintentionally alienating clients when they are already in pain.

Fourteen Things *Not* to Say

---
1. *"I'm so sorry"*

There are a number of reasons to eliminate this universal phrase from your repertoire.

≫ You join the conveyor belt along with everyone else. Because everyone says "I'm so sorry," it loses its impact, particularly when long lines of comforters come through the services to offer condolences. You want to be heard and to make a difference. This is not the way to do it.

≫ For most people, their first and most resonant context for the words "I'm so sorry" is as an apology for wrongdoing. That usage is so ingrained in us from a young age that when grieving clients hear those words, they trigger the internal psychological reaction of an apology. People are good at suppressing inappropriate responses, yet many mourners feel an urge to reply, "That's OK. It wasn't your fault."

≫ The phrase says something about how sad you feel but says nothing about the client. It may even prompt grieving clients to feel they need to comfort you instead of the other way around.

≫ Finally, it is a conversation-stopper because there is no good or comfortable reply. "Thank you" is the most common response, but that doesn't feel right. Most survivors resist the impulse to answer "So am I" or "Not half as sorry as I am." If a mourner does respond despite the awkwardness, then what happens? There is no opening for dialogue, and the interaction tends to stop there.

Saying "I'm so sorry" can and does express concern when you say it with sincere compassion. In surveys, mourners will sometimes say it was one of the most comforting things people said to them. However, when pressed further, it becomes apparent that "I'm so sorry" is comforting only because no one said anything better. You can offer greater, more genuine comfort that distinguishes you from the crowd.

2. "You have my sympathy"

As with saying you're sorry, this phrase is so omnipresent that it loses its impact. At least this time there is a logical response. You "gave" the grieving client something, so it makes sense to say "thank you." Unfortunately, you didn't really give anything except the knowledge that you care, a sentiment you can more effectively express in other ways.

3. "I know how you feel"

If you want to alienate grieving clients immediately, tell them you know how they feel because you are always wrong. Even if you've had a similar loss, you can't assume others approach it or experience it in the same way. An entire spectrum of factors determine a person's grief experience, including personality, prior experiences of loss, strength of support networks, grieving style, culture, faith traditions, particular relationship to the deceased, and more. The honest reality is that you don't know how they feel, and grieving clients unanimously resent it when you say you do.

4. "Time heals all wounds"

This well-worn phrase isn't true. Time puts distance between you and the event, but it doesn't heal anything. It is what you do with the time that heals. When you tell bereaved people time will heal them, you unconsciously encourage them to repress or deny their grief in the hope it will simply go away. This is the worst thing they can do if they want to reclaim joy in life.

5. "At least…" or "You should be grateful that…"

All mourners have things for which they are grateful. At the same time, they are deeply sad over what can no longer be. For instance, they may be glad that the loved one is no longer suffering yet sad because they will never hear that delightful laugh again. When you concentrate on only one side of the equation, you clearly telegraph that you don't understand their swirling mix of emotions. Your words minimize their pain. They learn you are just like everyone else—much more comfortable with the relieved and "happy" side of the experience and intent on cheering them up. From that point on, they suspect they can't be honest with you about their pain and sadness.

6. Anything having to do with business at the services

The services are definitely not places to conduct business, present a claim check, or try to set an appointment. Your sole purpose at the services is to express your care for your clients as people. Likewise, your initial card and contacts should be a forthright expression of your support and understanding, without mentioning your business dealings.

7. "Call me any time"

Hundreds of people say this; few honestly mean it. They do not want the grieving person to call any time, day or night, or to ask them for anything they might need. Besides, grieving clients are not going to call you. Grief saps their energy, making it difficult to articulate questions. They feel vulnerable and needy when they have to ask someone for help. They fear becoming a burden and do not want to intrude or impose. They simply aren't going to pick up the phone. You can tell clients to call you any time ... provided they are not grieving. For grieving clients, it is meaningless.

8. "You look good"

This is particularly applicable to clients who are seriously or terminally ill. People constantly tell them how good they look, hoping it will buoy the person's spirits. It doesn't, especially in cases where they cry when they look into the mirror themselves. They wonder what else you are not addressing honestly in your efforts to make them feel better. Even in those cases where they do look good right now, they know it won't last and they wonder whether you will still be comfortable with them when they look terrible. Overall, it's better not to place any focus on outward appearances.

9. There's nothing more that we can do for you

For clients with serious or terminal illnesses, these words are depressing and ominous. They are also false. Even when there is nothing medically that can cure an illness, there is still so much that can be done for your client—by you, a hospice team, the family, and more. All people can be helped to live as fully as possible until they take their last breath. This is an immense source of hope; don't snuff it out!

10. Anything that explains the loss or tells them their loved one is in a better place

There are five pertinent cautions here:

1. We don't know the answers or the reasons, and grieving clients do not want others to impose beliefs or rationalizations on them.
2. No explanation is sufficient to satisfy mourners or to justify their loss.
3. Tragedy and loss quite frequently knock the foundations of religious and personal belief out from under people (at least temporarily), and they need freedom and permission to grapple with those issues over time.
4. It can be risky to assure survivors their beloved is in a better place, particularly without full knowledge of the family "secrets" and backstory. Sometimes survivors are honestly not convinced of their loved one's present location.
5. Even when clients do believe their beloved is in heaven or has attained nirvana, at that moment it is hard to imagine a "better place" than right by their side on this earth. You risk unintentional alienation by your confident assurance of the deceased person's happiness.

11. "Should"

It is common for people to tell grievers what they should feel, how they should act, when they should clean out the closet or take off the ring, how they should handle their grief, and more. These well-meaning "shoulds" come from the unconscious ignorance of people who don't understand or who are not in the bereaved family's shoes. Do not "should" on mourners or tell them what to do and how to act. Do support and companion them as they trust their own instincts and follow their unique path to healing.

12. "Be strong"

This admonition tells grieving clients they are "weak" when they show anger, sadness, or tears. People need permission to embrace the full range of their experience, both positive and negative, and have that experience honored and respected. Telling clients to be strong, or agreeing with them when they say it themselves, is contrary
to healing, wholeness, and regaining joy. (See additional information on tears and repressed grief in the section Tears and Tissues on page 52.)

13. "How are you?"

It is difficult for a grieving person to accurately answer this query. Grief is such a volatile process of ups and downs that clients may feel differently from hour to hour. It's easier for them to dismiss it by answering "Fine" than it is to respond with a painful but honest explanation that would actually contribute to their healing. Besides, everyone they encounter asks this question, but grieving clients realize most of them don't really want to know. Therefore, they stick with the expected answer that offers no information, leads to no dialogue, and prevents effective support. "How are you?" isn't helpful—to them or to you.

14. "Put it behind you and get on with life now"

Grieving people are confused and offended by suggestions that place their loved one firmly into a box marked "Past" or that imply the way to move ahead is to forget. Instinctively, it doesn't seem right, nor is it consistent with research on grief resolution. Rather than putting the past "behind" them, the path to healing involves creating a memory out of what can no longer be and *taking it with them into the future.* The goal is not to "get over" or forget it; the goal is to assimilate the memories and acclimate to the loss in order to "get on with life."

15. Euphemisms

In our denial-prone society, we are afraid to use the actual words for death, illness, prognoses, and other "uncomfortable" transitions. We euphemize them beyond recognition as we dance around, add humor to, avoid, or try to soften the reality. While this may seem compassionate, the first step toward healing is facing and accepting the loss and its implications. When you use euphemisms, you participate in avoidance and let clients know you are like everyone else— more comfortable with denial than with painful but healing truth.

Be particularly vigilant to avoid euphemisms around children because they are concrete thinkers. If you tell them Grandpa went to sleep, they might not sleep peacefully again. If you say their beloved aunt expired, they will wonder about their own expiration date. If you say someone was called home, they won't answer the phone. Children need honesty, information you can explain on their level, and accurate words.

What *to* Say:
Twenty-Two Options That Comfort

Now that you know what not to say, what do you say instead? Some of these twenty-two options are useful during any transition. For more situation-specific examples, you can often modify the language to suit other transitions or losses. Regardless of the situation, every one of these offers comfort and helps build loyalty and trust that will last.

---

1. *"I can't imagine what this is like for you. Would you like to tell me about it?"*

This is an honest acknowledgment of the truth. It doesn't tell them you already know how they feel. Instead, it allows them to tell you about their experience so you might understand.

---

2. *"…How is it different?"*

If you have been through or know about a similar transition, this question offers a way to establish a common base of understanding while also allowing for the uniqueness of your client's experience.

Examples:

≫ If I were in your shoes, I think I would be in shock and walking around in a fog. Is that your experience, or how is it different?"

≫ "When my dad died, Mom said she didn't know what to call herself anymore. Is it like that for you, or how is it different?"

≫ "I recently learned that grief is often like a roller coaster of up and down, back and forth, and it sometimes feels like you take three steps forward and two steps back. Is it like that for you, or how is it different?"

≫ "Another client recently told me that so many people try to help, but they end up saying and doing things that are hurtful. Has it been like that for you, or how is it different?"

3. *"I know your grief won't be over in a week, a month, or even a year. Keep putting one foot in front of the other. Keep breathing. This will take a long time, and I'll be here for you."*

Most people at the services will go home within a week and stop calling shortly thereafter. Let grieving clients know you won't go away. You have more understanding and patience with their grief than others do, and they can count on you for the long haul. When you say this, of course, make sure you live up to your promises!

4. *"Healing doesn't mean 'getting over it' …"*

"Don't listen to people who tell you to "get over" this. Healing doesn't mean "getting over it" or forgetting. You heal by creating memories of what can no longer be and adjusting your life to the loss so you can move into the future. In fact, the greatest testimony you can give to those you love is to live a full life enriched by their memory. You will never forget, and you wouldn't want to. [Name] will forever be part of you."

This little nugget of education reassures grieving clients that what they've heard from so many other people is wrong. It brings relief to realize that they don't have to find a way to put their beloved in the past. They do have to let go of the physical presence of the person or thing they lost, but the separation is not thorough—their loved one remains with them and can enrich their life in the future.

In fact, there will never be a point of final closure, a time when your clients can say, "I will never miss her again. I will never cry again. I will never wonder what life would be like if she were still alive." For a significant loss, they will have "ambushes" or "grief bursts" for the rest of their lives. It may be triggered by something unexpected, as when someone who hasn't cried in years walks into a store, hears the person's favorite song playing on the public announcement system, and bursts into tears. Alternatively, it may occur in conjunction with anticipated events, such as when the classmates of a deceased child graduate from college or when a daughter walks down the aisle without her father. This is normal and healthy, as clients learn to let go of the physical presence but not the love.

5. *"Expect more volatility than the stock market."*

The grief process is not a linear progression where people gradually feel better every day, nor does it move neatly through pre-ordained "stages." Instead, it is up and down, back and forth, and often feels like three steps forward and two steps back. Your clients need reassurance that their recurring sad times and vacillating emotions are a normal and expected part of the healing process. In fact, the sad times often arise precisely because they are healing, as the reality and the practical day-to-day implications of the loss sink in.

6. *"I'll call you."*

Every time you contact grieving clients, let them know when you'll call again, and then do it. This way, they never have to wonder whether their questions are big enough to justify interrupting your day. They never have to muster up the energy and strength to call you. They know you will be there without them having to give it a second thought. This is refreshingly different from everyone else, and quite a relief!

7. "I'd like to help. Would you rather I run some errands for you, arrange for a caregiver so you can get out by yourself for a while, take you out to lunch, or do something else you need?"

When you ask grieving clients what you can do for them, either their minds go blank or they try to judge which things they believe you might be willing to do. Instead of making a generalized offer, list a few specific things. Clients then know they can choose from your list or name a similar request, with confidence that they aren't being burdensome or inappropriate. It also ensures that you will be helpful, while reinforcing that you understand more deeply than everyone else who simply asks "What can I do?"

8. "You have enough on your plate right now."

If anyone tries to bring up business at the services, deflect the attempt. This is easiest to do by saying "You have enough on your plate right now. Nothing has to happen today or tomorrow. I will make sure those things that have time restrictions or deadlines happen on time. For the next few days, just take care of each other and handle the decisions that are right in front of you. I'll call you next week when all the immediate tasks are over and you've had a minute to catch your breath."

9. "We don't understand why things like this happen."

Rather than attempting to explain away a loss, theologically or otherwise, simply admit the truth—we honestly don't know why things happen as they do. It's always better to let clients grapple with the questions and doubts on their own instead of offering a rationale that may not make sense to them or that may even alienate them.

10. "Death is not fair or logical, and it's always too soon when death comes to someone you love."

Death is unpredictable. It strikes young and old, fit and frail, and healthy and seriously ill. It does not abide by rules of equity, and its only logic is the fact that everyone will die.

Death seems particularly unfair and illogical when it comes early in life. Yet even when a loved one's death follows old age or infirmity, survivors mourn and miss that person. Clients wish their eighty-eight-year-old Grandpa could have lived to be ninety-eight. When it is someone beloved, death is always too soon. Clients are sad about the deaths, missing those who died and wishing they could have lived longer. Distinguish yourself from people who say "You are so lucky he lived such a long life" or other familiar (but ultimately unhelpful) comfort phrases. Acknowledge the ambiguity of death and their love for the deceased.

11. Break the tension and invite dialogue when clients tell you they are "fine."

"Fine" is the standard answer people give when they think you don't really want to know. Turn the word into an acronym, such as Frightened, Insecure, Neurotic, and Exhausted. Then add a little levity when clients say they are "fine" by replying, "Ooo, you know what FINE means, don't you? It means frightened, insecure, neurotic, and exhausted. I'm not so sure that's good." Then follow up by saying, "Besides, that's the standard answer people give when they think you don't really want to know. I honestly do want to know. I will always listen to the truth, even when it's hard. So would you like to tell me what's really going on?"

Use this whether clients are actively grieving, stressed out, diagnosed with a terminal illness, or going through any transition. It's amazing how often clients will chuckle, sigh with relief, and gratefully tell you what they are experiencing.

12. "I will do whatever I can as a professional to make this difficult process easier for you."

Grieving people can feel overwhelmed by complexity and often find it hard to concentrate on a paragraph in a book, much less a financial plan. This reassuring phrase—which can be said at countless points during a client's grief journey—admits your professional limitations while simultaneously acknowledging that your goal is to help make things easier and less complex. Then follow through with education, lists, frequent communication, and emotional support.

13. "It's normal to be relieved or grateful about some things and at the same time very sad about others. Most people bounce back and forth between the two. I just hope you are able to feel whatever you feel at the time without anyone else telling you what you 'should' feel."

When you say something like this, you give clients permission to experience both sides of the grief equation. Instead of telling them to always look at the bright side, be positive, or be grateful, you accept them where they are and allow a level of authenticity that many others simply can't handle.

14. "Our purpose together is to help you achieve your goals..."

"Our purpose together is to help you achieve your goals, and right now your goal is to heal, put the pieces of your life back together, and regain joy. I will make sure we keep track of all the financial aspects, but I am just as concerned about doing whatever I can as a professional to provide resources, support, and education for as long as it takes. I am here for you."

15. "You know, this wouldn't be so hard if you didn't really love her...'

Grieving people frequently berate themselves for not being "better" by now, especially with so many people telling them to put it behind them and get on with life now. Reassure them their grief is a normal reaction to losing something precious.

"You know, this wouldn't be so hard if you didn't really love her. Life can go on as usual when you lose something unimportant, but never when you lose a treasure. Your grief is a testament to your love, and there's no reason to be ashamed of that. At least with me, you never need to apologize for your tears or your grief."

16. "It's hard when people say hurtful things, isn't it? They mean well, and they are doing their best to be comforting. They just don't know any better. They haven't been taught, and they've never been in your shoes."

No one intends to be cruel or hurtful; they do the best they can. Yet, grieving people are frequently offended, alienated, shocked, or cut to the core by another's words or actions. Help your clients be patient with the attempts and hear the underlying expression of concern and compassion. This also reinforces the facts that you know better ways to help them and that they can rely on you to understand in ways that others don't.

17. Say the name.

Mourners want to know that others also remember their loved ones. They long to hear the name and share stories, even if it brings tears to their eyes. An old African tribal saying addresses this need: "No one is ever truly dead from this earth until there is not a person left alive who speaks their name or tells their story."

Don't be afraid to say the name, in person or on a card. Keep the stories and memories alive for your clients.

18. Say "died," "death," "cancer," "terminal illness," "died by suicide," "murder," etc.

An old proverb explains that "The beginning of wisdom is calling things by their right names." Using the proper words to describe what happened isn't nearly as harsh as people fear, and it is an honest recognition of your client's reality. Some clients resist using accurate words like death, died, suicide, cancer and so forth. Do not force them, but do not follow suit. When you have the courage to accurately name what happened, you let clients know they don't have to dance around it with you. This can be freeing for them and distinguishes you from all the others who avoid naming the reality.

19. "You're not crazy; you're just grieving. What you're saying/thinking/doing IS normal for a grieving person."

Bereaved people frequently feel that they're going crazy, especially when they face their first significant loss or transition. The intense, all-encompassing, and unpredictable nature of grief is a shock. They want to be "over it" … and are constantly told they should be. In fact, after the first few weeks, well-meaning people may suggest they need psychiatric medication. While it can be incredibly helpful for grieving clients to access a support group or grief coach, only a tiny percentage of people sink into diagnosable mental problems. Affirm and reassure your clients by normalizing their experience and letting them know they're OK.

20. "You are unlearning the expected presence of [name]."

We learn to expect the person, pet, or thing to be there as usual. The hardest times are when that expectation isn't met. For instance, grievers may instinctually pick up the phone to call the person and then realize no one will answer. Out of habit, they may call out a loved one's name when they come home or make the familiar trek to the pet food aisle. They see another person of similar build and hair color walking down the street and, for just an instant, believe it's their beloved. Grieving people have to retrain their brains not to expect the familiar presence, and that takes time.

21. "It's hard to let go of what you love. You want to go back to normal. But that normal is gone. Wherever this process leads you, I am here to help you build a new normal."

Although some transitions occur by choice, in many cases your clients are dragged, kicking and screaming, into a club they never wanted to join. They want their old life back and yearn for what can no longer be. Reinforce for them that there is no way to go back. The only way out is forward.

22. "You still have a future. It will just be a very different future than the one you planned."

Not only do grieving people feel they've lost what they cherished from the past, but they also feel they've lost their future. Actually, what they've lost is their dream for a particular future—their vision and plan for how the future was expected to unfold. Part of their task is to let go of those dreams and build new ones. This is easier said than done, but when you reframe it in this hopeful way, you help clients begin the gradual shift from looking backward and asking

"Why?" to looking forward and asking "What now?"

More Ideas

In addition to these twenty-two options, you can glean more ideas for what to say by reading through the suggested texts for condolence cards beginning on page 103. In addition to their use in cards, these words are appropriate on the phone, in a letter, in the office, or when meeting a client on the street.

When you use these skills and phrases, you let clients know you are truly listening in ways that most people don't. You help them heal. At the same time, when they believe you deeply understand and care about them, they give you their business and they stay for life.

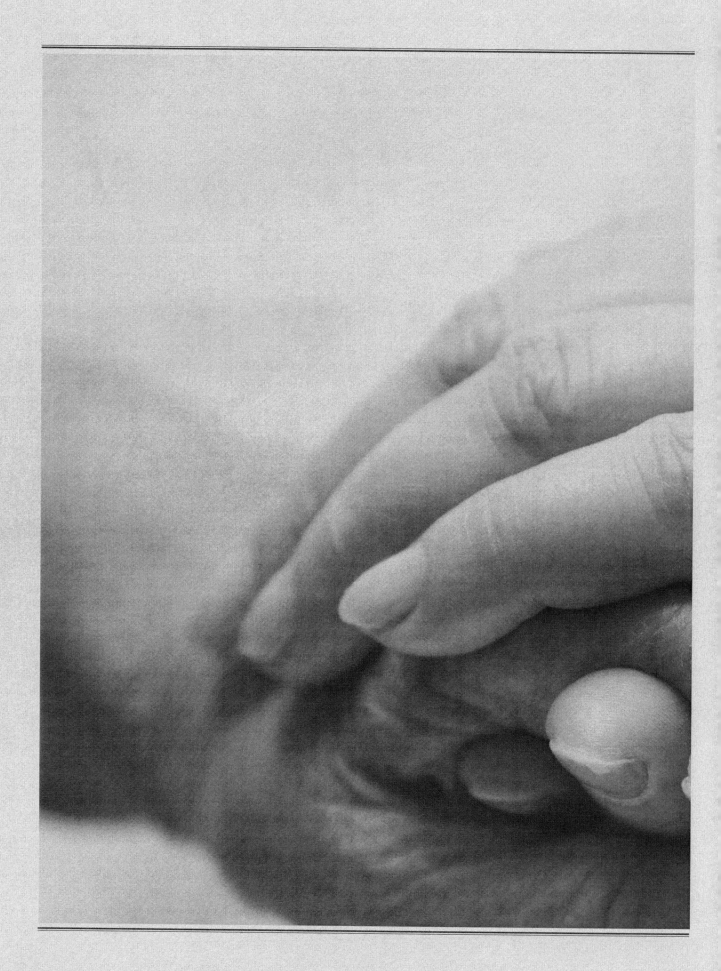

Eight-Step Protocol for Services After a Death

You're going about your day when you get the dreaded phone call. A client's family member died, and the services are tomorrow. What do you do?

Attend the services if you can. There's no substitute for personal presence. However, avoid being on the conveyor belt, going down the line saying "I'm so sorry" or "You have my sympathy." Offer real comfort in a memorable way.

Keep the purpose of post-death gatherings in mind: people come together as a family, as friends and community, to remember who they are, how they belong to each other, and how they will forever be different because this person has died. The services help them celebrate a life, recognize the death, and begin the formal goodbye.

Your reason for going to the services is to help accomplish these tasks. You are there to help remember and celebrate the person's life, let them know what you will miss, and offer reassurance that they are not alone as they say their goodbyes. Your purpose extends beyond paying your respects, doing your duty, and making an appearance. Everything you say

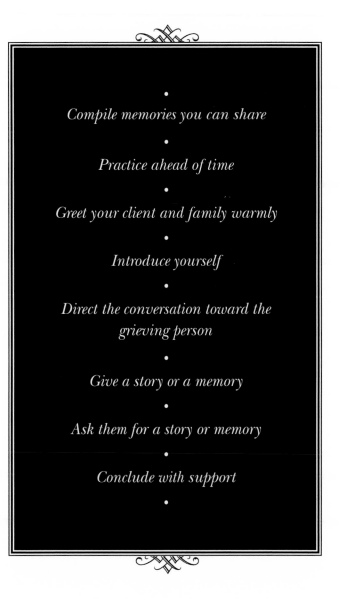

Compile memories you can share

Practice ahead of time

Greet your client and family warmly

Introduce yourself

Direct the conversation toward the grieving person

Give a story or a memory

Ask them for a story or memory

Conclude with support

and do needs to focus on the grieving family members and their needs, not on you.

If the grieving family is of a different cultural or faith tradition than yours, do research ahead of time so you understand their expectations and avoid offending them.

Use the following as a quick reminder of how to be truly comforting in a situation where so many others fail.

1. Mentally compile two or three stories and memories you can share.

If you knew the person well, this should be an easy task. If you didn't know the deceased person, read the obituary or other sources to glean the information you need. At the same time, mentally note the family members with whom you want to talk personally (e.g., a widowed spouse, the adult children, or siblings).

2. Practice ahead of time.

Running through scenarios in your mind is significantly less effective than role-playing aloud with another person. Enlist the help of a colleague, family member, or friend. Practice what you will say from the moment you extend your hand to your client. You want the words to flow easily and naturally without conscious thought on your part. After role-playing, you can reinforce it by speaking the words aloud in the car as you drive to the funeral home or church.

3. Greet your client and family warmly.

If you have a warm and affectionate relationship with the family or client, offer a hug. If not, give a two-handed handshake or place your free hand on the elbow or shoulder of the person you're greeting. Increasing your physical connection has a comforting psychological effect.

4. Unless you are absolutely sure the person knows who you are, briefly introduce yourself.

Grieving people can't think clearly and may have a hard time placing you. Remove any

awkwardness by reminding them of your name and connection. Then, so they know you are not introducing yourself in a business context, go immediately to the following step.

5. Name the reality and offer comments focused on the grieving person, even if you begin by saying something about yourself.

Examples:

≫ "I was so shocked when I found out Al died. I guess no one is ever prepared for news like that. If I was shocked, though, I can't imagine what this is like for you. What a tsunami!"

≫ "I don't like going to services like this; they are always so uncomfortable. But I came tonight because I care about you, and I cared about Frank."

≫ "Helen's death was expected, and yet when people actually take their last breath, it's always a shock. I came because I know it's not going to be easy for you, and I wanted to let you know I care."

6. Go on to give a story or memory.

Examples:

≫ "The memory of Sharon that I'll carry with me for the rest of my life is her big, infectious smile. Over and over again, I saw her walk into a room and start smiling. Soon, everyone else in the room was smiling too. She certainly knew how to make people happy. We are definitely going to miss that smile!"

≫ "I never met your father, but I was amazed when I read his obituary about how much work he did with the nonprofit organization. What a contribution he made!"

≫ "I'll never forget when Sheila came in to withdraw some money because she wanted to surprise you for your fortieth wedding anniversary. What a grin she had on her face!"

» "Keith could be pretty gruff, and not everyone found it easy to work with him, but under that gruff exterior, he obviously really wanted to do the right thing and protect his family. I really enjoyed working with him, and it was clear to me how much he loved all of you."

7. Ask for the client's story and start a dialogue. "But you knew her so much better than me. Tell me, what do you hope people will remember about Carol?" Then listen intently with good eye contact, and ask questions based on the story. Keep prompting dialogue as long as the client remains engaged.

8. End with support.
When you notice the client disengaging (e.g., looking at the people behind you, shifting weight from foot to foot, or tapping your hand nervously), simply glance at the line yourself and say something like, "There are many other people who want to talk with you. I won't take more of your time now. All these people are going to go home in a few days, though, and I know your grief won't be over in a week, a month, or even a year, so I am here for you for the long haul. I'll call next week just to check in, and I'll continue to do whatever I can as a professional to make this difficult situation easier for you."

Overall, do you see how this process is so much more authentic and comforting than going down the conveyor belt saying "I'm so sorry" or "You have my sympathy?" You truly support the grieving family members' needs, and they will remember you long after you're gone.

Other Family Members
There is no need to talk with everyone at the services. Concentrate on the list you formed in the first step.

Perhaps you've never met other family members, and you would like to speak with them. You can seamlessly make the transition as you leave your client's side. After offering your support, you can say, "Could you help me out here? I want to offer condolences to your children, but I have never met them. Could you point them out to me?" The client will respond, "Oh, of course. This is Tom, Kevin, and Susanne." You can then talk with the three of them together if you'd like, rather than going to each individually.

As you talk with other family members, repeat steps 1 through 8 with slight modifications to fit the relationship. For instance, you might say, "I just told your dad that my fondest memory of your mom is her big, infectious smile. It was amazing how she could walk into a room and get everyone smiling. Your dad and I agreed that we will all miss that. Your dad also said he hopes people remember her for her beautiful flower gardens and the joy they brought to so many people. Yet kids often have a different perspective than the spouse. Tell me, what do you hope people will remember most about your mom?"

Continue in this manner until you've spoken with as many people as you choose. It never hurts to stay a while, and with these steps in mind, you always have something comforting to offer.

A Note on Flowers Versus Donations, Cards, and Gifts Reconsider the practice of sending flowers to the funeral home. The plethora of flowers creates a problem for the family, since they rarely know what to do with them. Instead, create a more lasting legacy by using the money you would have spent on flowers to make a donation in memory of the one who died. Use any remaining money on cards, gifts, or flowers and send them throughout the first year and beyond. Gain suggestions for appropriate gifts and cards by reading through the texts for condolence cards, especially those for later in the year or on marker days. That chapter begins on page 103.

Delivering a Life Insurance Benefits Check

Every time an insured person dies, someone must deliver the claim check. Yet few people are skilled in doing so. In fact, many companies and agents of record simply mail the check with no personal contact whatsoever. Of course, in-person delivery is sometimes impractical, as when the beneficiary or multiple beneficiaries live in a different state than the decedent. However, when the processing and check delivery are done solely through the mail, beneficiaries feel no connection to the company or its representatives, and you miss a prime opportunity to offer genuine support, build inter-generational relationships, and retain clients.

You are notified of an insured's death in one of three ways, depending on your relationship to the client:

a. You receive a call from the client's family.
b. The company alerts you that it received a call from survivors.
c. You are assigned an orphan policy.

Regardless of the circumstances, you can incorporate skills discussed in this book to improve your delivery of life insurance claim checks. Note particularly the protocol for services and the skills to use when a grieving client comes into the office. In addition, here are a few key points:

1. Some insurance agents proudly tell me they are the only people who can bring a check to the grieving client at bereavement services. Unlike everyone else who comes in sorrow, these agents believe they bear good news and bring relief. They are wrong.

First, this is a private transaction. When you present the check in a public setting, you invite the curiosity and involvement of people outside the immediate family, thereby creating an awkward situation.

Second, what is the grieving person supposed to do with the check? Clients are not prepared to place such an important item in a secure place, nor should they be expected to do so. They will remember that you came to the services but that you caused a problem when you did.

Perhaps most importantly, when you proudly produce the check, you deliver the implied message that grieving clients should feel better because now there is money in their hands. Even if the funds relieve anxiety about paying bills, grieving family members would rather have their loved one by their side than any amount of cash. Suggesting otherwise feels crass and hollow, especially at that moment.

2. Although you will not bring the check with you, do attend the services if possible, even if you do not know the family or the deceased. Your purpose is to offer genuine comfort using the protocol outlined in this book. There is no substitute for your personal presence and sincere words, especially when you offer them without an associated business task.

3. If you are not able to attend the services, leave a voicemail or, if someone answers, make the call very brief. Introduce yourself if necessary. Tell them you will do everything you can to make things easier for them in this difficult time. Then give the day and approximate time when you will call to check in, see how the family is doing, and begin attending to the business necessities. Reassure clients that the process is specifically set up to meet their needs, and you will

advocate for them as you walk through it at their pace.

4. Call at the time you proposed. When you talk with family members, use these skills:

a. If you could not be present at services, begin the phone call with the steps discussed in this chapter for attending them–introduce yourself, say something about the deceased, ask for their memories, etc.

If you did attend, remind survivors of your presence by mentioning something about the services, and reinforcing that you heard and remember the family stories. For instance, "I can still hear that inspiring hymn from the funeral. What a great tribute to Sean. As you said, we will remember his self-giving nature and his willingness to try anything."

Then ask open-ended questions, i.e. "As you think of the services, what stood out for you or what did you most appreciate?" Invite survivors to talk for as long as they remain engaged.

b. When the conversation winds down, gently switch to business and let them know you are being straightforward with them by saying, "I'd like to explain the entire process of what will happen with the life insurance benefit so you know exactly what to expect." Then, in recognition that grieving people lose concentration, follow this up with "Don't worry too much about remembering every detail because I will be here to walk you through the whole process and advocate for you. I just want you to know up front what will happen."

c. Explain to survivors that you will gather data now to get the claims process going. In a few days, they will receive a packet with information and a one-page form to complete. You will call when that packet arrives and answer any questions. Whether over the phone or in person, you will assist in completing the form and ensure it is returned correctly. When the claim is processed and the check arrives in your office, you will deliver it personally, answer any further questions, and set up an appointment at the beneficiary's convenience to explain options for going forward.

If personal delivery is impossible, tell survivors you will deliver the check via certified mail and follow up with a phone call, during which you can answer questions and set up a phone appointment or video conference to explain options for going forward.

d. Ask whether the client has any questions so far. If not, begin collecting information for processing the claim.

e. End the phone call with support, reassuring survivors that you will be there through the entire process and beyond, because you know their grief will not be over in a day, a week, or a month.

5. Whenever possible, deliver the check in person. Although everyone knows the purpose for your visit, do not begin with business. Instead, incorporate open-ended questions and invite the story. For instance, you can say, "I imagine this week has been a whirlwind for you. What has it been like? What do you wish people knew about what you're going through?" Another helpful query: "I've talked to hundreds of grieving clients, and they tell me that what they most clearly remember from the services are the stories they heard about the person who died. What stories and memories did you hear that were meaningful for you, or was your experience different?"

Questions like this are not intrusive. They invite grieving family members to tell their stories, keeping the focus on them rather than on you. Remember always to follow the client's lead. Some clients won't want to talk much, if at all, though they will know you began with compassionate inquiries. Most grieving clients are eager to talk, especially on the topics just mentioned. Listen attentively and ask follow-up questions based on what they say. Allow plenty of time.

6. When the conversation winds down and it is time to deliver the check, avoid all suggestion that this will make things better. Instead, say something like, "There is nothing in the world and no amount of money that could take away your sadness right now. I only hope you can receive these funds in the spirit that [name] intended and as a gift to take care of your needs while you put the pieces of your life back together in the coming months."

7. Offer to discuss options when the client is ready. "If you are interested now, I can explain some options for the use of these funds going forward. Or, if you are like most people and aren't ready yet, I'll be checking in every week or so and we can talk about it any time you wish."

If the company has provision for a checking account or other method of temporarily keeping the proceeds safe and accessible, you can modify this to say, "It may seem like science and financial regulations have nothing to do with each other. In cases like this, though, psychological studies and financial regulatory authorities agree that no one, personally or professionally, should be putting pressure on you to make big decisions immediately. Other than things with specific deadlines such as estate tax filings, there is wisdom in allowing time for the fog to clear before making major or irrevocable decisions. Besides, any major

changes right now just add to your grief, and that's the last thing you need. So don't let anyone pressure you. All the money is safe and you have access to whatever funds you need. I will check in every week to see how you're doing. When you are ready, we can evaluate a number of different options that will protect your financial future and honor [name]'s legacy. In the meantime, just take one day at a time. Give yourself room to breathe, so we can make wise decisions going forward."

8. Close with support: "I know your grief will not end soon. It never does when someone you love dies. If you have any questions you can certainly call me, but know that I will contact you regularly. I'll be here through the entire process and beyond, doing everything I can as a professional to make things easier for you in this difficult time."

9. Make sure you follow up with a card, phone calls, and perhaps a small gift. For example, on the 6-month anniversary or on a birthday, send a card that says, "I know I can't take away the pain, but I hope you can at least enjoy a cup of your favorite coffee with the enclosed gift card." Another alternative: "Many people by now have stopped bringing up [relative]'s name or talking about [him/her]. Yet I hope you keep the memories alive by saying the name and telling the stories. After all, a life may end but love never does." Find many more suggestions in the chapter on condolence card texts.

In summary, regardless of whether this is an orphan policy or one of your own clients, avoid the easy route of mailing the check without any personal contact. Instead, go the extra mile. Attend the services, using procedures that fit your relationship to and knowledge of the deceased person. Whenever possible, deliver the check in person and follow up with regular contact. The grieving family will never forget it.

When you follow this protocol for delivery of insurance benefit checks, grieving clients perceive you as compassionate and wise. You are there for them as people rather than simply discharging a duty. You bring the financial support that could prove vital as they move forward, yet they know you are concerned about more than just their money.

When a Grieving Client Comes into the Office

When you know clients are grieving, schedule extra time for listening to their stories and experiences. This is never wasted time; it is an investment in the relationship and fosters a healthy professional intimacy. Think about how much time, energy, and money it takes to acquire a new client. Spend that time, energy, and money on your grieving clients, and you will retain them for life plus earn referrals to family, friends, and associates.

Implement the following ideas for your meetings with every client in transition and grief:

Setting the Appointment

If you have an administrative assistant or receptionist who answers your phone, begin there. After all, no matter how proficient you may be with grieving clients, you can't apply your skills if the person who answers your phone alienates them.

Typically, financial professionals set client appointments around their own availability. To the extent possible, reverse the protocol for grieving clients, who will deeply appreciate the

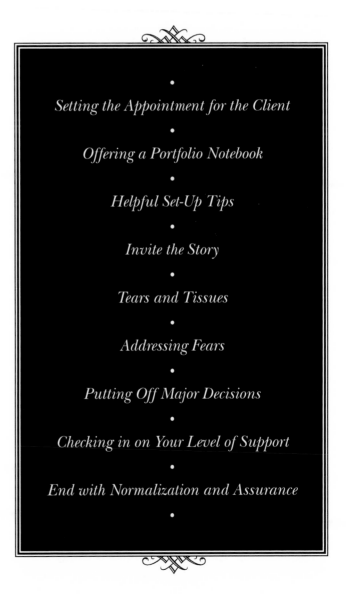

Setting the Appointment for the Client

Offering a Portfolio Notebook

Helpful Set-Up Tips

Invite the Story

Tears and Tissues

Addressing Fears

Putting Off Major Decisions

Checking in on Your Level of Support

End with Normalization and Assurance

consideration you show during a time when their life is in disarray.

In addition, let them know you have some expertise that most other professionals lack. The lessons in this book provide you with basic training in the needs of grieving people and how to be sensitive to them. You may wish to further that training with our multi-day class or other training opportunities and adjust your presentation to clients accordingly.

Imagine this scenario: A client refers a widowed friend to your office. When she calls to request an appointment, your staff member responds: "I'm glad you called, and I am happy to help you with an appointment. It may be reassuring for you to know that in this office, we go beyond just financial matters. We have specific training in the unique issues faced by people in transitions like yours and are more knowledgeable than most professionals you encounter. In fact, let's start right away. Why don't you tell me the days and times that work best for you? I'd like to arrange this appointment around your calendar if I could."

Offering a Portfolio Notebook

In the best of times, it's hard for people to keep track of their policies, agendas, action steps, and so forth. For grieving clients, it can seem overwhelming. A portfolio notebook is a thoughtful gift to assist them in that task. You may wish to give this gift yourself, or you may wish to extend the client's introduction to your services by having your receptionist or administrative staff offer it when the client comes in for the first appointment.

This is one possible script for your staff:

"Good morning. It's so nice to meet you in person. [Advisor's name] asked me to give you a gift that many of our clients find helpful.

You will be covering a lot of information in your meetings—reading documents, signing paperwork, creating action steps for your next meeting, and more. Frankly, it's hard to keep track of it all even under normal circumstances. Many of our clients find it helpful to use this portfolio notebook. Notice that it has a pocket for papers, a three-ring binder, a notepad, and even a pen—everything you need for your appointments with us. Then you never have to wonder where everything is, what you signed, or what you have to do before we meet again. It's all right here in one place. Many of our clients find it helpful, and you can use it that way, too. Here is your gift from [advisor's name]. Now, could I get you a glass of water or something else to help you be comfortable?"

At this point, prospective clients have not set foot into your office or met you, yet what are they thinking about you? Even if they choose not to use the notebook in the way you envision, the thoughtfulness of your gift will impress them.

Helpful Set-Up Tips

≫ If you're meeting with a grieving couple, place their chairs close together with nothing in between, so they can hold hands or offer support to each other without having to move.

≫ Place a clock on the back wall or in a location where you can see it but they cannot. Then, they never see you visibly checking the time.

≫ Place some signs of life in the space (e.g., a water feature or plants).

≫ Provide "comfort foods" in small dishes with accessible small napkins (e.g., regular and diabetic chocolates, pretzels, almonds, or popcorn).

≫ Have a box of tissues on your desk within easy reach of your clients.

≫ Consider having handheld gadgets like a Rubik's cube, twisty toys, silly putty, etc.

Some clients like to have things to "play with" when talking about difficult topics. Even if no one uses them, they contribute to a more relaxed atmosphere.

≫ In case clients forget, make sure you have a copy of all necessary documents, extra pens, and anything else they'll need for the meeting.

Invite the Story

Although professionals fret about what they should say to grieving clients, it's more important to ask good questions and then actively listen to their answers.

The most important need these clients have is to talk about their experiences and tell their stories. It helps them process and begin to accept the reality. Sadly, within days or weeks of a significant loss, few people are willing to listen to the story anymore. Instead, others start instructing grievers to "put it behind them and get on with life." Wherever they go, there's a big white elephant in the room and everyone tries to avoid, ignore, or peek around it.

If you don't bring up the topic, you fit in with all the others who cannot name the reality. Although you may get business done, there will be an awkward and uncomfortable aspect of your meeting, and grieving clients will leave your office feeling unsettled. At home, they are constantly inundated with advice telling them who to engage for their needs. Will they have a compelling reason to stay with you?

Remember, tens or even hundreds of thousands of professionals can do the work you do. Clients give business to those who understand their lives.

During your interactions with grieving clients, consistently ask open-ended questions that invite their story and then follow their lead.

In other words, open a door and give clients freedom to walk through the door or to close it. Most of the time, they will walk through the door and tell you the story because they hunger for someone who will listen.

Even if your clients choose not to accept your invitation, you differentiate yourself from all the others who fear raising the topic, the big white elephant disappears, and the tenor of the entire encounter changes. In addition, your clients are free to reopen the door later because you let them know you are comfortable with their grief and willing to listen. You have nothing to lose by asking good questions. You potentially have a client to lose if you don't.

The following are helpful questions that invite clients to talk. In many cases, the answers also give you valuable information so you can better serve their needs.

• "Before we even get started on business, this has to be one of the most difficult things you've ever been through. Would you like to tell me what happened or what you're experiencing now?" (This gives clients an option of whether to answer with facts and actions or with a general emotional sense. They are more likely to answer when your invitation includes their preferred way of telling the story.)

• "What do you wish people knew about what you're going through?" (Listen carefully to the answer because clients will tell you what they wish you knew.)

• "How do you wish people would act around you?" (Clients will tell you how they wish you would act around them.)

• "Who are the most supportive people around you, and what are they doing to support you so well?" (This informs you of their trusted network, whom you may wish to bring into the process and/or you may be able to gain as clients in the future.)

- "In what ways has the reality sunk in, and in what ways does it still just seem unreal?" (Continue to ask this question for months afterward because it takes a long time to recognize both the reality itself and the full implications of the loss.)

- "What has surprised or shocked you about this experience?"

- "When are the toughest times for you?"

- "How do you handle the tough times, and what practices have you found to be most helpful?"

- "What do you most want and need from me right now?"

- "At our last appointment, you said you felt [like a strand of blown glass]. Is that still true, or what has changed since then?"

- "What kind of day has it been for you today?" (This is better than "How are you today?")

- "Your family members are grieving too. Which of them seem to experience it similarly to you? Which, if any of them, are good talking companions for you?"

- "Are there any people in your circle you're worried about, and if so, in what ways?"

- "What kinds of things went swirling through your mind when you got the news?"

- "Now that you're a bit down the road in this process, what advice would you give to other people who find themselves in similar situations?"

As you ask these questions, practice active listening. Lean toward clients and keep good eye contact. Nod your head and encourage them with occasional affirmative phrases and sounds like "Uh-huh," "I see," "That must have been hard," or "Mmmm."

When you are meeting with more than one person, make a conscious effort to include everyone in the conversation. You can do this by looking directly at a person who has said little and say, "Shelley, not everyone has the same experience in these situations. Is your perspective like Tom's, or in what ways is it different for you?" Then continue looking at Shelley while she answers. If Tom interrupts, politely say, "Hold that thought, Tom. I'll get back to you in just a minute. Shelley, you were saying?"

When clients pause in the story, three effective skills invite them to continue. For illustration purposes, assume the client said, "When the doctor walked into the room, I could tell by the expression on her face that the news wasn't good."

a. Restate what the client said. "So when you saw the expression on the doctor's face, you knew it wasn't good?" Then pause, and the client will pick it up from there.

b. Rephrase the client's words with added details. "So when you saw that expression on the doctor's face, you got scared and braced yourself?" or "It sounds like the clue to brace yourself for bad news was written all over her face?"

c. Request more information. "What kinds of things were racing through your mind when you saw the doctor's expression?"

These queries lay a good foundation you can build on over time. Continue to ask open-ended questions based on what your clients tell you so you can continue to serve them effectively.

Questions to Ask during Positive Transitions

Even positive transitions trigger grief. Although clients are excited and happy about moving to another chapter or experience, they always have to leave something behind. Be the wise advisor who recognizes both sides of the emotional equation.

The following are examples of questions to ask during some of life's most common positive transitions:

a. **Retirement:**
   - "It's wonderful to finally reach retirement, but you have to leave a lot behind as well. What do you miss about your old life?"

   - "We've almost achieved your goal: you will soon retire! That is thrilling, and yet closing a major chapter in your life often triggers sadness or regrets. What is the anticipation of retirement like for you? Are you thinking about what you will leave behind, even as this new, exciting chapter awaits?"

   - "Many people approach retirement with mixed emotions, but they may be reluctant to acknowledge it to people who are envious or who tell them how lucky they are. What do you wish people knew about what the experience is like for you at this point?"

   - "Sometimes people are happy to let go of the stress of their job, but they miss the regular interaction with their colleagues. Is it like that for you, or how is it different?"

b. **Marriage:**
   - "It is a wonderful thing to marry the person you love. We have to admit, though, that there are advantages to being single. Recognizing that there is an element of grief involved does not mean you don't love your spouse or that you regret getting married. In fact, it helps you deal with your marriage better if you honestly recognize what you no longer have. So as you move into this new and fulfilling chapter of your life, what things are you sorry to leave behind?"

   - After listening, you can then ask, "Now, tell me again, what is it about [name] that makes it worth it for you to leave those things behind?"

c. **The birth of a baby:**
   - "I know you've been looking forward to having a family for a long time. Parenting is not easy, though. Taking a guess, I imagine you miss things like a good night's sleep or the ability to go out without carrying a minor U-Haul. Is that right, or what have you found challenging about having a baby?"

   - "What has surprised you most about having a baby or being a parent?"

   - "If you were writing a piece of advice for couples who are pregnant right now, what would you tell them about the experiences you've had since your baby's birth?"

   - "Having a child can change the entire family dynamic, including relationships with extended family. That isn't always the case, though. Have you noticed any changes in your immediate family or extended family?"

d. **A new job or promotion:**
   - "Starting a new job is exciting, but I imagine it is a challenge too. You have new responsibilities, higher expectations, and different colleagues. Would you like to tell me what things are fun and interesting

about your new position and what you miss about your old one?"

- "This job has caused big changes in your life. What do you see as the major differences, both positive and negative?"

e. A move from one city to another:
- "It's normal to have mixed emotions about such a significant move. You are moving to something good, yet you have to say goodbye to so much. Would you like to tell me some things that you will miss?"

- "Some people find it useful to honor their memories when they move away from a place they have cherished. Have you thought of any ways that you can tangibly take memories with you? For instance, you could take pictures of yourself in all the locations that have been special to you and fashion them into a memory booklet. Before you leave, perhaps you could set up a trip to come back so you can visit your old friends and eat in your favorite restaurant. Maybe you'd like to take pictures of each room in your home, take little snips of the carpet fabric, or take some of the window treatments with you. Does something like that make sense, or what other ideas appeal to you?"

Use these suggestions as a guide, modifying them for various situations and relationships. Be there for your clients in all transitions, both positive and negative, with uncommon understanding and skill.

Tears and Tissues

Most of your clients and colleagues have grown up believing that tears are a sign of weakness. Consequently, when a person starts to cry in the presence of others, he or she often apologizes for the tears. Commonly, you will hear, "I just have to be strong," which translates into "I can't show my emotions or cry."

In this context, we inaccurately define the word "strong." It takes a great deal of energy to stuff tears down and keep those emotions deep inside. It takes true strength to face and express the pain, acknowledge the vulnerability, and face the void that can never be filled in the same way again. In reality, the strong person is not the one who doesn't cry; the strong person does.

Besides, tears are nature's stress-relief mechanism, containing physiological chemicals that relieve stress. That's why we call it a "having a good cry." (Interestingly, the tears that stream down your face when you slice an onion have none of the stress-relieving chemicals. They only occur in tears of emotion.)

Finally, repressed, denied, or ignored grief does not go away. It remains and eventually finds a means of expression. We may experience physical symptoms such as headaches, neck aches, backaches, and stomachaches. We may experience outbursts of anger, impatience with someone who doesn't deserve it, or even clinical depression. Sadly, repressed grief may result in a life never fully lived again because of the fear of ever risking one's heart.

It is healthier to face grief and allow tears, both in yourself and with your grieving clients.

Tears are especially problematic for men in our death-denying society. Many of them are raised to deny emotions and never shed a tear.

Yet, many men do need to cry and benefit greatly from permission to do so. As noted in the discussion on grieving styles, some men (and women) cry a great deal, while others cry very little.

As always, you follow your client's lead. Give permission and encourage facing the emotions, reassuring clients of confidentiality, and then allow them to choose their response.

What does all this mean for you in your office?

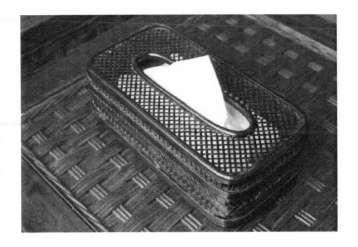

Suggested protocol:
Our most instinctual response when someone cries is to hand that person a box of tissues. However, there are two reasons why that is not the best practice. First, it takes grieving people out of control. They are compelled to take the tissues to be polite, regardless of whether they want them. More importantly, extending the tissue box gives an unintended message: "Stop it. Dry your tears. Use this. You are making me uncomfortable." In support groups, grieving people call the box of tissues the "shut-up box!"

Instead, keep a box of tissues on your desk within easy reach of your client. When tears well up, casually lean back, nod at your tissue box, and say, "You can use my tissues if you want; it's up to you."

Then follow up by saying some or all of the following: "People think they need to apologize for their tears. They think they're being 'strong' when they refuse to cry. They're wrong. You show such strength and courage when you face the pain and difficult emotions. It's not the strong ones who don't cry; it's the strong ones who do."

Besides, tears are nature's stress-relief mechanism, and we all need less stress! We've built our entire relationship around helping you achieve your goals. Your biggest goal right now is to get through this, heal, and find joy in life again. My office is a safe and confidential place. When you are here, you don't need to spend energy stuffing down emotions that need to come up. You never need to apologize for your tears. In my office, you can cry any time."

A final note: Some professionals fear that giving their clients permission to cry will result in a nonstop flow of tears. Actually, when people have permission to cry, they usually need to cry less. When they do cry, they may relieve enough stress that they're better able to focus on the business at hand. Most importantly, they learn you are a trusted resource who understands them in ways most other people don't.

Addressing Fears

Grieving people always have money worries, especially when the transition has a negative impact on their finances. In fact, a widow's greatest fear is ending up on the street as a bag lady. In some cases, the fears may be rational. If the fears are rational and clients may run out of money, you have serious work to do. Yet in most cases you encounter, the fears are irrational.

Many professionals attempt to soothe irrational fears with logic. They show charts and graphs illustrating the investments, interest rates, and withdrawals, believing that if clients see "proof" of their safety, they will no longer be afraid.

Unfortunately, it doesn't work. Fear can arise regardless of whether the trigger is logical. If you doubt that, show a high-resolution picture of a snake to someone who is terrified of snakes. Logic dictates that the picture is no threat, but the person is powerless to squelch the visceral, fearful reaction.

Instead of using logic, effectively address your clients' fears with the following steps:

First, invite the fears: "Everyone in your situation has fears about their money. Let's put them out on the table. What keeps you up at night? What worries you about your financial situation? What is the worst thing that could happen to you financially?"

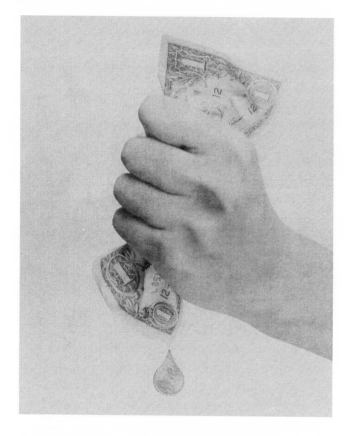

You can help clients through the process by creating or purchasing note cards, each of which names a common fear. Place them on the table and ask which ones resonate most and why. Offer some blank cards so clients can write additional fears. (If you get a consistent addition from several clients, make a new note card containing the additional fear.)

Ask clients to say more about why they chose each card. Listen carefully as they speak, clarifying to make sure you understand each fear: for

example, "What I hear you saying is this ... Is that accurate, or how is it different?" As you ask questions and listen, help clients prioritize their top two or three money worries.

Research shows that naming, writing down, and writing about fears objectifies them and takes away some of their emotional power. It helps move fears from the emotional center of the brain to the more deliberative area, which helps clients think more clearly and feel less threatened. Therefore, your next step is to instruct them to write down their top two or three money worries. The portfolio notebook mentioned above may be useful here.

Then say, "Since these are the worst things that could happen to you, what can we do together to help keep you safe?"

Brainstorm ideas together. Even if you already know good solutions, lend credence to their ideas or state your strategies in terms that match their suggestions. When you have the top "safety" strategies, instruct the client to write those down on the same page as the fears. Perhaps the fears can be on the left side and the strategies on the right. Make a copy to keep in the client's file.

Conclude by saying, "Now take this list home. Every time those fears rear their ugly heads, day or night, take out this list. Look at your fears, look at what we're doing to handle those fears, and be reassured that you are safe."

Putting Off Major Decisions

It is generally accepted wisdom that grieving people should put off major decisions, especially irrevocable ones.

This is sage advice for two important reasons. First, the "fog of grief" brings lack of concentration and an inability to clearly think through decisions and their implications.

Countless grieving people make decisions they later regret. (And if clients have regrets later, whom will they blame?) This "fog," combined with the exhaustion of grief, also means clients are less able to withstand pressure from others, particularly family members, who insist that they make decisions before they are ready or who wish to take advantage of the situation for their own benefit.

Second, every transition triggers grief, especially if it involves any break in attachments. If clients make major or life-changing decisions (such as selling their homes), they invite additional pain at a time when they are already hurting.

Therefore, follow this protocol. During your first meeting with grieving clients, make a list of the time-restricted things that have to happen and when (e.g., estate tax filings, trust funding deadlines, etc.). Present the list to your clients and say, "These are the things that must happen on a particular schedule. Let's look at them together so you are aware of them. Then rest easy because I will ensure we get them done on time."

Follow up with this: "Other than these things, psychologists tell us it's a wise idea to put off making major decisions for a while, especially when they are irrevocable. I agree. When anyone is grieving, concentration and rational thinking aren't as keen as they need to be to make major decisions. Besides, do you need any more grief in your life? Whenever you make major changes, you pile more grief on your plate. So let's do a thorough review to make sure we're not missing anything, and we'll continually assess your situation along the way to make sure everything is in order. Other than that, you have a right to wait a while. Don't let anyone pressure or push you into making big decisions. You won't regret waiting; you might regret acting too soon. Keep taking one step at a time. We'll get there together, and we'll act only when you are fully ready to do so."

Checking in on Your Level of Support

On occasion, you'll encounter clients who prefer not to be reminded of their loss or to hear the beloved's name. They may be in denial. They may be unable to process the grief and are trying to push it down. They may have developed a pattern of reacting to grief by forgetting and starting new. They may prefer to grieve strictly in private rather than discussing it with anyone else, especially in a professional situation. In short, there are a variety of reasons why a particular client may wish you to stop being so "supportive."

You can easily check in with a client during a meeting. For instance, you can say, "I've been sending you cards, mentioning [name], and acknowledging the depth of your loss. Many people find those steps to be supportive, but not everyone. My goal is to serve you the best I can, so I'd like to check in on this. Of the things I've been doing, what do you find helpful, and what do you wish I would stop doing?"

You can also ask, "What do you wish I knew about your needs right now?" Listen well, and adjust your practices to your client's desires.

End with Normalization and Assurance

Even if you spend the majority of a meeting listening to stories and tears rather than accomplishing concrete business, always reassure clients that you accomplished good things together. Tell them it's important for you to understand their experience so you can serve their needs, and thank them for trusting you with all aspects of their lives rather than just their money. Let them know it is a privilege for you to get to know them better and to support them during this difficult time.

Emotional Differences Between Divorce and Widowhood

Some issues facing divorced clients are similar to those facing widowed clients. Their entire social networks have changed, and former friends (especially coupled friends) often drop away. People don't know how to support them or what to say. The impact on finances is often negative. Divorced and widowed people no longer have a partner to discuss issues with. Both need to build new identities as single people, including deciding which last name to use and checking off a different "marital status" box on forms. They have to answer awkward questions about what happened. They have to deal with the grief of their children as well as their own. They have to unlearn the expected presence of the other, let go of what can no longer be, and build a new and different future.

Despite all the similarities, there are differences. One particularly common loss during divorce is intrapsychic: the shattered dreams of the happy marriage and family that clients envisioned as they walked down the aisle. Questions about self-image and lovability often exacerbate the pain.

Although there are exceptions, the level of anger also tends to be higher with divorce than with widowhood, since a widowed spouse is less likely to blame the other person or think of the death as a betrayal. Anger can be especially prominent in situations where one spouse surprises the other with a divorce decree or the breakup involves contentious factors, such as an affair, substance abuse, or fights over custody.

Finally, divorced clients have to contend with a still-living ex-spouse, so they can't close the door on that chapter of their lives. At least for a while, every communication can be a painful reminder that reopens wounds or causes new ones.

Interestingly, research shows that when an ex-spouse dies, the grief of the survivor can be profound. A complex level of attachment remains, even in the most contested divorce cases. Additionally, the children of the former union experience a parent's death, with all the implications and complications that a loss of this magnitude entails.

You will need to fully implement the skills in this book in cases where both members of the couple choose to retain you as their financial advisor. If you agree, be proactive to ensure you are not caught in the middle. Explain that you will not be on one person's "side" or hide information from one or the other of them. You will act objectively with each of them and with both of them together to help them make the best decisions possible. You will coordinate referrals to other experts if there are issues that go beyond your purview, and you will maintain the highest ethical standards as the divorce proceeds.

If the couple is uncomfortable having the same financial advisor and one chooses to go elsewhere, pledge to collaborate in whatever ways are helpful. Keep the door open for the future as well, explaining that once the divorce is final, all business dealings and conversations with either of them become completely confidential again. Even if one or the other chooses to work with someone else until that time, you value your relationship with each of them and hope you can serve them in the future.

No matter where your clients are in their divorce process, they need your support and understanding. All of the strategies and skills in this book apply equally to the grief of divorcing couples. Continue to ask open-ended questions and listen well during what is sure to be one of the toughest times of their lives.

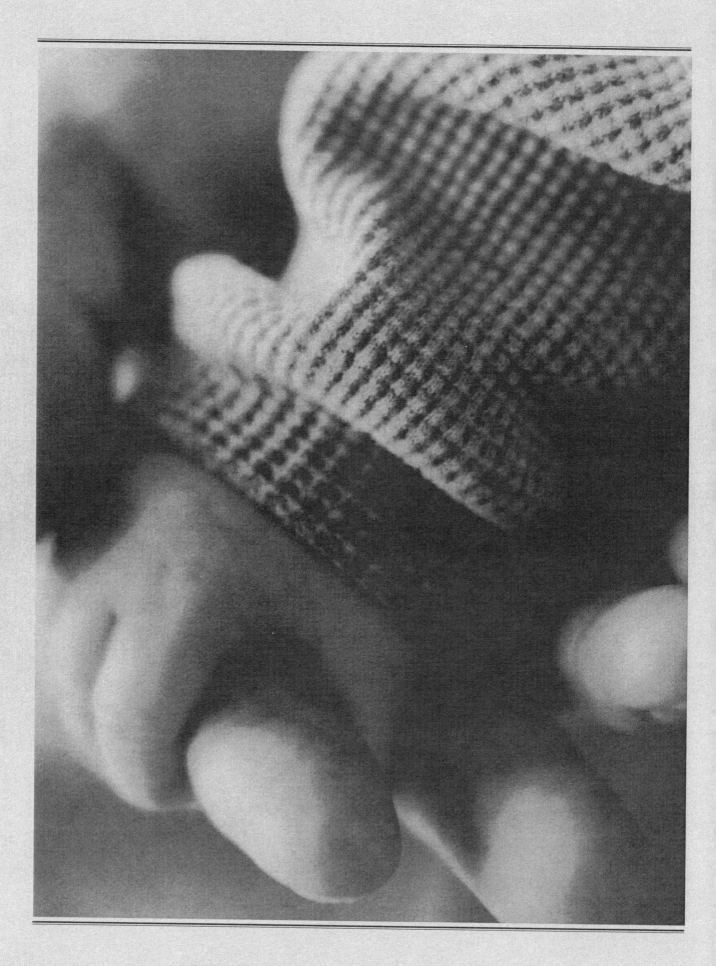

Special Issues

Clients needing professional help

It's often incredibly helpful for people in transition to talk with an objective, knowledgeable person who can help them get through with greater grace and ease. If you suggest this to everyone, no particular client gets the impression you believe something is wrong with him or her; it is simply your standard advice. Therefore, make it your protocol to recommend grief coaches, counselors, and support groups to every grieving client. Not everyone will take advantage of these services, but many clients and/or their family members will. Those who do will thank you.

How to compile a list of services:

» Call area hospitals and hospices, which often provide a variety of bereavement support services
» Call area churches, which provide support groups themselves and/or have lists of resources to which they refer their members
» Call colleges with pastoral counseling or counseling degrees and ask for the names of top graduates in the field of grief counseling

» Ask clients who have experienced a trauma or loss for the names of people or groups that were helpful to them
» Watch the newspaper for notices of support group meetings in your area

Create an attractive brochure from the data, complete with contact information. When you offer the brochure to clients, say something like, "I give this list to every client in your situation because grief and transition are hard on everyone, and healing takes a long time. It can be invaluable to talk with an objective and knowledgeable person who isn't going to judge you or your experience and who usually has helpful strategies to try. In fact, it seems to me that people who take advantage of resources like counselors and support groups get through the experience easier and faster than those who don't. Who knows? Even if this list isn't useful for you, someone in your family might appreciate it. So here you go. For what it's worth, this is a list of resources we've found useful for all of our clients who are experiencing life transitions."

At subsequent meetings, follow up by letting clients know you're always refining and improving your list of resources. Ask them whether they've accessed services or read books that were helpful to them and are willing to offer you their feedback. This noninvasive inquiry provides you with information for your resource list while facilitating your follow-up with that client.

On occasion, you will encounter clients who need more help than a support group or grief coach can offer. For instance, they may sink into clinical depression, which requires psychiatric intervention and potentially anti-depressant medications. While every grieving person experiences deep sadness, trouble sleeping, lack of energy, and decreased enjoyment, diagnosable clinical depression is persistent, occurs continuously for at least two weeks, and interferes with the person's ability to function normally. Here are some signs to watch for:

» Being unable to get out of bed in the morning (No one who is grieving really wants to get out of bed, but some people truly cannot.)
» Neglecting personal hygiene and appearance
» Gaining or losing weight rapidly
» Significant change in personality
» Losing interest in everything and everyone
» Talking about suicide (Many bereaved spouses or parents say they wish they had died instead or they wish they had died with their beloved. This is normal. Take further action when someone talks about taking his or her own life, especially if the person has a plan for how to do it.)

If you notice the above signs, talk to your client about seeing a psychiatrist to help him or her get back on track. Also, contact the family, express your concerns, and recommend that they arrange for professional help. Document your observations and each conversation so you have a record.

Luckily, extreme cases are rare indeed, and immediate family members often handle those that do occur without your involvement. Still, it's good to be aware of signs indicating that normal grief is crossing into the realm of clinical depression or complicated mourning, which require outside help.

When the Loss Involves Young Children

As a professional, you won't be directly responsible for a child's grief, but it's helpful to have basic knowledge so you can assist clients with young children.

In the past, conventional wisdom said that kids are resilient and if you leave them to their own devices, they'll be fine. It isn't true. Even young children mourn for what or whom they lost, and they need information, support, and attention.

When adults try to "be strong" for their kids by holding back their own tears and emotions, kids get false messages.

When children feel confused, hurt, and sad but observe adults acting as if nothing happened, they begin to fear that something is wrong with them. They may wonder whether other family members truly loved the person who died or whether they were just pretending as long as the person was alive. (This can lead to wondering whether they themselves are loved and whether anyone would miss or mourn for them if they died.) They learn that to be grown-up, they need to repress their feelings and deny their grief.

With all these confusing and conflicting messages, children can feel isolated and alone. They worry about the tsunami of emotions that they experience but dare not express.

Loving adults need to attend carefully to grieving children. If they answer questions at a child's level and help children learn at a young age how to grieve in healthy ways, those children will grow into more competent adults.

For your clients to answer questions at a child's level, you may wish to give them insights from Maria Nagy, a major researcher on children's grief. Here is her brief description of death concepts by age:

» Under 5 years old

Children under five have a limited ability to understand death. They perceive the dead person as living somewhere else. They do not conceive of death as irreversible or definitive but as something that can be reversed. Separation is painful, and they want to go visit the person wherever he or she lives now. They ask repeated questions about where the person is or when they can talk to the person again. They commonly report seeing the dead person or talking with him or her; adults should ask them to talk more about it instead of attempting to talk them out of it. They need reassurance, information, and answers to their questions as often as they ask.

» Five to nine years old

Children at this age realize they cannot go visit a dead person, and they gradually come to understand that death is irreversible. However, they don't perceive death as inevitable for everyone. Death is outside or separate from them—a "thing" that can "get you." They may become afraid of images like the Boogie Man or Grim Reaper. Some exhibit exaggerated fear of the dark, or they may regress to an earlier stage of development (e.g., wetting the bed or sucking a thumb). They may get angry with someone who died because the person failed to escape fast enough, allowing Death to catch him or her. They often engage in games that allow expression of their

confusion and emotions. In fact, you can learn much about children's perceptions by observing their play or playing with them. Children at this age need reassurance, security, and love instead of punishment for their grief symptoms.

» More than nine years old

Abstract thinking progresses enough by this age that children can perceive death as universal, irreversible, and realistic. Separation is intensely painful because they know it cannot be alleviated. They may try to act "grown up". Yet despite their best outward attempt to mimic the "strong" (and therefore misguided) behavior of adults, their feelings inside are raw, persistent, and especially confusing. They may be angry if they believe the person who died did something avoidable that contributed to or caused the death. They may have many questions about the facts of the death, and their questions need honest answers or they will invent scenarios that are worse than the truth. They need to talk to someone they trust—often someone other than a parent. They need to mourn, express their feelings, create enduring memories and connections, and learn how to go on without the one they loved without forgetting.

Overall, the best way to help kids deal with death and grief is to prepare them ahead of time. Even young children can observe dead animals, leaves falling from trees, and the cycle of life. It's best for parents to encourage questions about what death is and what happens to a dead body.

Ideally, young children should be taken to services for people they don't know well, so they can get all their questions answered in an emotionally neutral environment. Then, when someone they love dies, they don't need to ask big questions about death, bodies, and caskets because they already know the answers. Instead, adults can concentrate on the child's emotional needs.

A caution against euphemisms: children are concrete thinkers. If someone tells children that a loved one went to sleep, they will not sleep peacefully. If they are told someone expired, they will wonder about their own "expiration date." If they hear that someone was called home, they will fear answering the phone. Adults need to use real words and answer questions honestly, starting with a brief explanation and progressing to more detail as the children ask more questions. Death should be an open topic, while always following the child's lead.

Children rarely grieve constantly, tending to alternate bursts of grief with playtime. They need permission and even built-in play breaks so they can forget for a while. Actually, that's not a bad strategy for adults as well. It's helpful for everyone to have times of respite and relaxation in the midst of grief.

Just as you researched resources on grief for your adult clients, gather information on the child grief services that are available in your area. You can check with many of the same organizations and facilities. Many hospice organizations and hospitals offer support groups for grieving children of various ages, and plentiful grief counselors specialize in children.

Consider giving clients books and resources that may help their kids, especially resources with journaling and child-centered grief activities. You can check the bibliography in this book for resource ideas. You can also use or recommend websites like http://www.hospicenet.org, http://www.dougy.org, http://www.griefnet.org, and http://www.compassionbooks.com.

Suicide

A few sobering statistics:

≫ Suicide is currently the third leading cause of death in the United States for people aged fifteen to twenty-nine.

≫ Someone in the United States dies by suicide every seventeen minutes.

≫ Although elderly people die of too many chronic or terminal illnesses for suicide to be a leading cause of death, the suicide rate per capita is higher for those over age eighty-five (especially widowed white men) than any other age group.

≫ The suicide rate in soldiers and ex-soldiers is also alarmingly high and continues to grow. In the Iraq-Afghanistan war, more soldiers died by suicide than died in combat.

≫ Only a quarter of suicide victims leave a note, so the majority of survivors may never know why their loved ones took their own lives.

≫ Grief over a suicide is more long term due to the stigma and complications involved. In fact, studies show it can take three to five years for acute grief to subside for a parent whose child dies by suicide.

A note about terminology: Psychologists increasingly caution against saying "committed suicide." We commit murder, larceny, or other crimes. While suicide may be "a crime" in the figurative sense, in literal terms it is a tragedy with complex implications. So when you talk to clients, instead of saying "committed suicide," use the term "died by suicide" or "took [his/her] own life."

Research shows that people who die by suicide do not want to be dead. They want to be out of pain and see no other way to escape. In other words, the pain exceeds that person's resources for dealing with the pain. In the vast majority of cases, there is a diagnosable mental problem, such as clinical depression or bipolar disorder, often combined with enough abuse of alcohol or drugs to numb the strong human instinct to live.

Problems may go undetected because a suicidal person can become expert at hiding pain and abuse, frequently due to the fear of disappointing others, of being a burden, or of being exposed.

Therefore, although it is sometimes obvious beforehand when a person is deeply troubled, in many cases, suicide catches families completely off guard and they cannot understand why it happened. Survivors may be wracked with guilt that they didn't know more, missed or failed to heed signs, or couldn't prevent it. They reel with anger at the person who died and the perceived insensitivity of the act. They can be overcome by embarrassment and shame, and they wonder what other people will assume about the family or the situation. Because of the stigma and obvious discomfort most people exhibit when the topic is raised, grieving survivors are reluctant to admit or talk about what happened.

When you talk with clients after a suicide, take the following steps:

» Do not be afraid to name the reality, noting the terminology suggested above. When you name it first, you let clients know they can talk honestly with you without mincing words, which is something they don't often find.
» Avoid all the unhelpful phrases previously discussed, such as "At least she's no longer in pain." Ask open-ended questions and listen well, but take care not to ask why the person might have decided on suicide, whether there was a note, or how the client makes sense of what happened. All of those questions induce more guilt than comfort.
» Do relate stories and memories if you knew the person who died, or ask for stories and memories from your clients.
» Acknowledge the normalcy of swirling emotions of guilt, anger, shock, and grief.
» Gain more ideas on what to say by reading the texts for condolence cards following a suicide. The overriding principle is to ask good questions and listen deeply to the answers.
» As with all your grieving clients, ensure that you have a reference list of support groups and counselors in your area. Survivors of a loved one's suicide benefit from support groups and professional help even more than most grieving people. They especially need to express and deal with their guilt, anger, and musings about what else they could have done to prevent it. Remind clients that it's not a sign of weakness to talk with someone who better understands their experience. In fact, it is often immeasurably helpful to have someone else light the path for them.

On occasion, you may encounter clients who speak of taking their own lives. Always take suicidal talk seriously. Although many grieving people wish they too had died or wish they didn't have to deal with life without the loved one, you need to be watchful for those truly at risk. Ask directly whether it's just wishful thinking to imagine joining the one they love or whether they think they could actually do it. If they could do it, ask whether they know how they would carry it out. If a client has a plan in mind, the risk is extremely high.

Even if they don't have a plan, whenever you're concerned, get help. Call family members. (See the discussion on letters of diminished capacity in the section titled "Your Office Protocol for Dementia" beginning on page 81, so you have permission to make these calls.) Know of resources in the area for counseling suicidal people and for immediate at-risk intervention.

For a seriously suicidal client, call the national hotline at 1-800-SUICIDE together, and don't let your client leave your office without a companion. Then follow up to help ensure he or she gets treatment and isn't left alone.

Several helpful organizations offer education and support, both for prevention and for support of families after a suicide:

American Foundation for Suicide Prevention:
http://www.afsp.org

Suicide Prevention Lifeline:
http://www.suicidepreventionlifeline.org

Suicide Prevention Services of America:
http://www.spsamerica.org

Suicide Prevention Resource Center:
http://www.sprc.org

National Institute for Mental Health:
http://www.nimh.nih.gov/health/topics/suicide-prevention

American Association of Suicidology:
http://www.suicidology.org

Murder or Violent Death

Survivors of murder often receive tremendous sympathy, even from strangers. While this may be comforting, survivors also lack privacy because so many people recognize them as the family of a murder victim. Especially in high-profile cases, they can feel their own lives are stripped away as well.

The levels of denial and shock are greater after a murder than after an accident or natural death. The concept that another person's decision can snuff out an innocent life seems incomprehensible. Survivors are commonly tossed by waves of anger at the injustice and unfairness of their situations and at the murderer personally. They speak of their loved one as stolen or ripped from their grasp. If the murder was particularly heinous, they may have nightmares imagining their loved one's final hours or minutes.

Police investigations, pretrial hearings, and the drawn-out process of seeking a verdict complicate the grief process for murder survivors. Each hearing, especially if it involves evidence, pictures, and stories of the crime, is another blow, throwing them back into the vortex of pain.

During a judicial process that can take years, suspects may remain free, and it is immensely painful for survivors to encounter them or hear of their normal activities of life. Sometimes a perpetrator negotiates a plea bargain to a lighter sentence or the verdict is "not guilty." Sometimes the murderer is never found. All these factors complicate the grief process.

Even a guilty verdict with a resultant prison sentence or death penalty does not provide closure to the grief because it doesn't begin to address the loss of the person who died. Murder survivors sometimes are caught in the web of trying to understand murder rather than attending to their grief. They focus so much on who the perpetrator is, why the perpetrator committed the crime, how it could have been prevented, what is required for "justice," and other issues surrounding the murder that they don't take time to acknowledge, accept, and work through their personal loss.

In almost all cases of murder, survivors cope better when they receive professional help and/or attend support groups. They need understanding, compassion, hope, and the assistance of others to avoid being trapped and suffocated in the mire.

As for other complicated cases, do the research to discover resources for your clients. Offer a good book on this type of grief (see the bibliography in this reference guide for starters). Ask good questions and listen well. Send a card or give them a call on the day before or after every court hearing. Say the name of the person who died, use the word "murder," and be a safe,

confidential, understanding person your clients
can trust.

Helpful websites:

Families after Murder:
http://www.familiesaftermurder.com

Support after Murder and Manslaughter:
http://www.samm.org

"Homicide Survivors—Dealing with Grief,"
a comprehensive PDF created by the Canadian
Resource Centre for Victims of Crime:
http://www.crcvc.ca/docs/homsurv.pdf

Documents Every Client Should Have

Background Information

Increasingly, clients seek out professionals who understand their lives so they can give them their business. They want your financial assistance, but they also want help in protecting themselves and their loved ones in ways that go beyond the monetary realm. They want to build a meaningful life, fulfill their goals, and pass on financial and nonfinancial legacies to their survivors. In fact, research shows that clients of firms who regularly include "legacy conversations" in their service offerings perceive the firm's value to be ten times greater.

If you'd like to be ten times more valuable to your clients, this chapter gives you the information and tools you need to become a truly comprehensive, sought-after firm. When you facilitate the completion of the following documents, you help clients stay in control of decisions even when they are incapacitated, protect those they love, and pass their wisdom on to future generations. You become the hub at the center of a wheel of essential resources, and your clients will appreciate and enthusiastically refer your holistic service to others.

Some of the documents listed below are legal forms requiring consultation with an attorney. If you are not an attorney yourself, develop a network of referral partners you can trust. You may even choose to accompany valued clients to their first meetings with these professionals. At the least, follow a protocol in which you refer clients to an attorney, follow up to ensure the documents are completed, and keep copies of everything.

We recommend that you use or subscribe to a service offering a digital lockbox. This is a secure account folder in the cloud that your client can access with a password. Some broker-dealer platforms, firms, and software programs (e.g., eMoney) include a digital lockbox as a feature. Ensuring documents are prepared and then keeping them in one secure location establishes you as an invaluable resource and the go-to person for clients and for their families.

The Most Important Documents

This table lists the advance planning documents every client should complete

NEED	SOLUTION
Documents in which clients express wishes and desires so their choices may be honored even when they are temporarily or permanently unable to make decisions for themselves	1. **Living will and/or Five Wishes** 2. **Physician Orders for Life-Sustaining Treatment (POLST Paradigm)** 3. **Durable power of attorney for health care** 4. **Durable power of attorney for property/finance** 5. **Do not resuscitate (DNR) or do not intubate (DNI), if applicable** 6. **Organ donor registry**
Documents that enable clients to give assets to the people they choose and provide financial protection to persons or entities	7. **Last will and testament (often coordinated with trusts)** 8. **Life insurance**
Documents that facilitate passing on wisdom and life lessons	9. **Legacy will/Ethical will** 10. **Other legacy instruments**

1. Living will/Five Wishes

This advance directive lists the treatments clients do and do not wish to receive in various circumstances. Contrary to political rhetoric and common misunderstandings, living wills are not designed to "pull the plug on Grandma." In fact, Grandma may request every treatment known to humankind, no treatment, different types of treatment for different conditions, or whatever she chooses.

Every state has its own version of living will, with or without addenda that allow for more expansive explanations. A living will is more useful when it is as specific and as detailed as possible. Ideally, it includes the rationale behind the choices; since it is impossible to describe every medical situation, knowing why the client desires a particular treatment is more instructive than the description of the choice itself.

A completed living will is not legally binding. Family members can still disagree, and when they do, the family's desires usually prevail with medical professionals. Nevertheless, a living will remains the clearest description of what clients want. It greatly increases the chances their wishes are carried out, especially if a case goes to court.

An increasingly popular form of living will is the Five Wishes document. Available at http://www.agingwithdignity.org, this form goes beyond medical choices. For instance, it includes comfort wishes such as religious icons clients find comforting, the type of music they'd like played in their room, whether they want regular massages, etc. It also includes a section listing what they want family members to know. The form guides clients through questions that help them think about their options and is a more comprehensive and useful document than a state's standard living will form.

Forty-two states accept the Five Wishes document as a stand-alone living will. In the other eight states (Alabama, Indiana, Kansas, New Hampshire, Ohio, Oregon, Texas, and Utah), it is accepted provided it is attached to the state's standard living will form.

Consider giving a Five Wishes document to every client. Purchased individually, they cost $5 each. Purchased in quantities of twenty-five, they are $1 each. In quantities of 1,000, they can be co-branded. This is an inexpensive but valuable way to add value and demonstrate your concern for clients.

2. POLST Paradigm Forms

POLST is an acronym that stands for Physician's Orders for Life-Sustaining Treatment. Some states have a different nomenclature (e.g., MOLST, MOST), but all the variations fall under the umbrella of a POLST Paradigm Form. This newest addition to the living will arena is not yet available in all states. As of March 2013, the following states had endorsed POLST Paradigm Programs in place: Colorado, California, Hawaii, Idaho, Louisiana, Montana, New York, North Carolina, Oregon, Pennsylvania, Tennessee, Utah, Washington, West Virginia, and Wisconsin. The only states that had not begun developing a POLST program were Arkansas, Mississippi, and South Dakota and the district of Washington D.C. All other states were in the process of developing their forms. You can find current information, including an up-to-date map of states with approved forms, at http://www.polst.org.

One major difference between a POLST and other living will forms: clients discuss the options with their doctor, and both the client and the doctor sign the POLST Paradigm form. Therefore, it becomes a doctor's standing order and can be entered into the person's permanent

medical record. Your client's wishes thus possess the enforceability of a doctor's order, and they are available whenever and wherever the medical records are accessed, subject to Health Insurance Portability and Accountability Act (HIPAA) privacy laws.

A second innovation: Medical professionals who follow POLST directives in good faith cannot be sued for doing so. This removes the medical professional's reluctance to follow your client's wishes in situations where family members disagree or where the recommended course of action is unclear.

In other words, POLST Paradigm forms lend significantly more gravity, enforceability, and accessibility to a client's living will. The POLST Paradigm form is especially helpful for a person nearing the end of life, as it combines the living will with a DNR/DNI order (discussed below).

Since the POLST Paradigm deals exclusively with medical issues, encourage clients to complete both a Five Wishes document and a POLST form. If there are any contradictions between the two, the POLST takes precedence because it is a doctor's standing order.

3. Durable Power of Attorney for Health Care

Also called a health-care proxy, this document names the person(s) responsible for making health-care decisions if a client is unable to make them, either temporarily or permanently.

Recommend that clients name at least one alternate in case their first choice is unable or unwilling to serve. For instance, many people choose their spouse, but if a couple is in a car accident together, they cannot serve for each other. In addition, the closest relative may be unable or unwilling to make the tough decisions required in some circumstances.

Regardless of whom your clients choose, it is crucial that the designated person be fully informed of your client's wishes and the reasoning behind those wishes. The rationale is perhaps even more important than the actual choice. This information enables the person to make decisions without guilt and second-guessing.

You provide an invaluable service if you arrange this meeting in your office. Bring the parties together, invite the client to read the forms aloud, and then facilitate discussion until the health-care proxy thoroughly understands the client's wishes and intent.

4. Durable Power of Attorney for Property/Finances

This document names the person(s) authorized to make financial decisions if clients are unable to do so. This is essential for gaining access to accounts and being able to withdraw, spend, and handle finances for incapacitated clients.

Unlike the health-care proxy form, the durable power for property/finances may require periodic renewal to be enforceable, and different entities may require their own version of the documentation. Inform yourself about which of your client's investment custodians require their own versions of the durable power of attorney and how often they require updating or re-signing. (For instance, some custodians and banks require re-signing every six months.) Do what you can to ensure that the person(s) of choice can access and manage your client's finances.

5. Do Not Resuscitate (DNR) and Do Not Intubate (DNI) Orders

Resuscitation, with or without intubation (referring to a ventilator tube and respirator) is the only medical procedure universally applied without permission to anyone whose heart and/or breathing stops. Medical personnel automatically administer it unless there is an order to the contrary.

Obviously, healthy clients would not have DNR or DNI orders; they would want to be resuscitated and hopefully returned to normal functioning. However, the elderly or frail, persons with dementia, or those in the advanced stages of terminal illness may decline resuscitation or intubation if their heart or breathing mechanisms fail. For patients in these situations, resuscitation is successful only 5 to 15 percent of the time. Even when the attempt succeeds, it is a physical procedure that often causes deep bruising and broken ribs, which can add to the patient's pain.

Your clients may wish to complete these forms if they are terminally ill because they want to die of the heart attack if it occurs rather than be resuscitated only to face imminent death anyway, potentially with increased pain. Perhaps clients no longer want mechanical interventions so they can die peacefully with family attending to them rather than with frantic hospital staff attaching machines. Clients diagnosed with dementia may wish to put into their living will forms and instruct their health-care proxy that when they reach a specified stage of incapacity they do not want resuscitation or intubation. Other clients, of course, may want every attempt possible to keep them alive, no matter their condition. This is an individual decision but an important one.

A final consideration: These documents are useless if they are not accessible. Redundancy is your ally. Clients need to keep copies in their medical records, near their front door, posted on the refrigerator or freezer door (emergency personnel are often instructed to check there), posted above their bed, and on the door to their room. Remember, unless emergency personnel see the forms, they will act to resuscitate and/or intubate.

6. Organ donor registry

As of 2013, eighteen people die every day awaiting organs, and the rate keeps increasing. One person who donates organs can save the lives of eight other people. A tissue donor can improve the lives of fifty people. Many organ donors and their families view the donation as a way to bring meaning out of a tragedy or allow the deceased person to give life to others.

This also is an individual decision. Some faith traditions do not allow organ donation. Some people simply can't embrace the concept. Others make decisions based on the circumstances of the death.

If clients wish to donate organs, most people believe signing a driver's license is enough. That is not necessarily true. Many states require family consent, so family members can override the client's wish. In addition, sometimes the driver's license is not available to medical staff when they need to make decisions.

The best way to make these wishes legally enforceable and accessible is to sign the state's organ donor registry. Each state has its own registry but also honors the registries of other states. You can get more information and find the form for your client's state at http://www.organdonor.gov. Because this form doesn't require an attorney, clients can sign the registry in your office if they choose.

After signing the registry, it's a good idea for donors to also sign their driver's license and carry an organ donor card.

7. Last Will and Testament
This foundational document is a legally binding way to pass assets and possessions to survivors, identify heirs and executors, name guardians for minor children, distribute or manage a financial legacy, reward or punish survivors, and more.

Your clients may use a will in conjunction with one or more trusts to minimize estate taxes, keep assets out of probate, and retain more control over distributions even after death.

Except in the simplest cases, it's best to involve an estate-planning attorney in the preparation of a last will and testament.

Subsequently, review your clients' wills on a regular basis to ensure they are up-to-date and still express their wishes, especially when there are changes in family relationships or the client's financial situation.

8. Life Insurance

Clients purchase life insurance to provide money (the death benefit) for the named beneficiary when they die. The primary objective is to help clients protect the people they love from negative financial impact.

Insurance vehicles vary widely, allowing for fulfillment of a broad spectrum of goals. Insurance companies calculate premiums based on age and health and the policy's type and duration, frequency of payment, and amount of death benefit. When you understand your clients' needs and goals, you can structure life insurance appropriately for those purposes, with the primary aim of protecting their loved ones in the event of death.

If you need to involve an insurance agent or firm in the process, refer clients to someone in your referral network, follow up to ensure policies are in force, and keep copies in your office.

9. Ethical Will or Legacy Instruments

When people are given the choice of passing on a financial legacy or conveying their wisdom and life lessons, they overwhelmingly choose the wisdom and life lessons. They want to know their life made a difference and that they will be remembered. They want to teach descendants hard-won lessons from their own lives, in hopes of improving the lives of the next generation. They want their spirit and guidance, rather than only their money, to live on in palpable ways.

Therefore, although these documents have no legal standing, they are relevant and powerful.

There are countless ways to pass on life lessons, stories, and wisdom. They may incorporate the written word, audio, video, or a combination thereof. Regardless of format, the intent is to convey whatever your client wishes to hand on.

In addition to the aspects of legacy writing included in the Five Wishes document, these are examples of a few of the many published resources for legacy instruments:

- Barry K. Baines. *The Ethical Will Resource Kit,* 1998. http://www.ethicalwill.com/kit.html or 877-827-7323

- Jack Reimer and Nathaniel Stampfer. *So That Your Values Live On: Ethical Wills and How to Prepare Them.* Longhill Partners, Inc., 2009. http://www.amazon.com/So-That-Your-Values-Live/dp/1879045346. This book is written from the Jewish perspective but is usable in any context.

- Scott Farnsworth and Peggy R. Hoyt. *Like a Library Burning: Sharing and Saving a Lifetime of Stories.* Legacy Planning Partners, 2008. The book is available from several sources, including Amazon at http://www.amazon.com/Like-Library-Burning-Sharing-Lifetime/dp/0971917779.

- Marty Hogan. *Telling My Life's Story: The Caregiver's Guide to Conducting a Life Review with the Hospice Patient.* Sacred Vigil Press, 2011. This small booklet is a useful guide for families or caregivers to help dying people record life stories and wisdom. http://www.sacredvigil.com/booklets/booklets/telling-my-life%E2%80%99s-story.

- Donna Pagano and Jeff Scroggin. The Family Love Letter, http://www.familyloveletter.com.

10. Other

Other types of memorial instruments are widely available. Religious beliefs, culture, personality, and many other factors influence your clients' preferences and decisions on these possibilities.

This brief listing of some options can help you be aware of the broad range of alternatives:

- Letters, notes, or videos intended for a later date. For instance, a parent may create something to be viewed or read when the kids graduate from high school or college, when they marry, and/or when they have children of their own. Clients may create a different one for each child or grandchild, or they may wish to convey personalized messages to specific people. Videos carry the added benefit of allowing survivors to hear and see their beloved ones, thereby maintaining memories.

- Scrapbooks with pictures, mementoes, and stories of a person's life.

- Thumbies: A pendant created out of the thumbprint of a person who is dying or aging. Thumbies are available from many sources in gold, silver, pewter, platinum, or other metals.

- Tribute blankets weave a picture of the person (alone or with others) into a blanket typically used as a throw blanket, a bed covering, or a wall hanging. One supplier is http://www. PhotoWeavers.com.

- Cremated remains, despite the term "ashes," are bone fragments largely made of carbon that can be used in a variety of ways. Client reactions to these ideas will range from delight to disgust, so carefully gauge their level of interest in this type of option.

  - Simulated diamonds or other gems: LifeGem was one of the first companies to create these stones, but a number of vendors now compress and process cremated remains to create crosses, hearts, Celtic knots, rings, earrings, pendants, and more. Check http://www.lifegem.com and other sites.

  - Memory paintings or blown glass: Some people wish to keep cremated remains in their home. If that is their choice, they have options besides keeping them in an urn. Cremated remains can be crushed finely and incorporated into paint used to create whatever picture is desired by the family—a portrait, landscape, favorite vacation spot, favorite flowers, wedding scene, etc. The remains may also be incorporated into blown glass and formed into a vase or bowl. See http://www. CremainsArt.com.

  - Source material for coral reefs: Cremated remains provide a means to enrich ocean life when they are injected into coral reefs. This helps some people feel they are contributing to the environment. See http://www.eternalreefs.com.

- Memorial videography: A number of companies help families create meaningful videos. They may create a montage of interviews with the dying person while he or she is still capable. They may create movies from the past and present, a video of still pictures, or a documentary of the person's life. The finished product may take different forms designed to convey the intended wisdom, lessons, and messages or simply aspects of the person's life. Sometimes the family shows these videos in the funeral home.

The possibilities for these ethical and legacy instruments are as large as one's desires, imagination, and goals. Introduce the idea of passing on life wisdom, lessons, and a lasting legacy with your clients, offer them possibilities, and follow their lead. Help your clients decide what best fits their situation so they can create customized versions to pass on a legacy.

11. A Final Recommendation

As you store all of your clients' documents, wishes, and instruments in one place, consider including all the pertinent information their survivors will need in the event of their death or disability. This list includes the following items:

- » Passwords to all online accounts
- » Social Security number
- » Veterans Administration information, if relevant
- » Name and contact information of employer
- » Name and contact information of all banks where accounts are held, and all bank account numbers
- » Active credit card accounts, including the account number and phone number
- » Location and number of a safe deposit box, the location of the keys, and a listing of the contents
- » Name and contact information of insurance agents plus all policy numbers (life, property, health, disability, long-term care, etc.)
- » Net worth statement
- » Name and contact information of all debtors and loans (both given and received, including mortgage and home equity loans)
- » Name and contact information of lawyers, especially estate-planning attorneys

- » Copies of birth and baptismal certificates, marriage certificates, divorce or adoption papers, passport, and driver's license plus the location of originals
- » Descriptions of make and model of cars, car titles, and the usual location of car keys
- » Information and deed of the cemetery plot, if applicable
- » Location of post office box and keys, if applicable
- » Location of income tax returns and contact information of the preparer
- » Name and contact information of regular doctors, dentists, and medical facilities

Gather this information and keep it securely in the lockbox with client documents. Update the contents with your clients at annual review meetings and whenever their life circumstances or relationships change.

One final step increases your connection with the next generation. On your letterhead, compile a list similar to the one above of all the information held in the lockbox. Recommend to clients that they send the list to adult children and anyone else who would need to contact you and gain access to the information after clients die. This ensures that the family learns of your comprehensive service and establishes you as the person who can provide everything they need promptly and efficiently.

To Remember or Not To Remember: Is It Dementia?

There is increasing concern about the possibility of dementia in clients, and rightfully so. One in eight people over the age of sixty-five and half of those over eighty-five have some form of dementia. Financial professionals need education about the condition. They also need to know how to prepare in ways that protect both the firm and the client, what signs to watch for, and what to do if there are suspicions of diminished capacity.

Forgetful Clients

Forgetfulness, especially in older clients, isn't a sure signal of dementia. Some memory lapses are part of the expected aging process as neurons and synapses change.

In addition, there are two categories of non-dementia causes of forgetfulness:

≫ Medical causes: for example, a vitamin B-12 deficiency; some disorders of the thyroid, kidney, or liver; certain infections; interactions of medications; and more. These are all diagnosable and treatable, usually resulting in a return to full function.

≫ Psychological causes: for example, the grief process triggers impairment in concentration and memory. Full function will normally return as the fog of grief lifts.

Finally, mild cognitive impairment (MCI or amnestic MCI) is an interim or permanent condition in which people are more forgetful than is typical for their age, yet they do not have dementia. A higher percentage of people with MCI than without it do go on to develop dementia, and a great deal of research is focused on preventing that deterioration. However, some MCI patients remain stable at that level and live out their days as the stereotypical "absent-minded professors."

Clients with Dementia

An important clarification: Dementia is not a disease in itself; rather, dementia is a condition caused by one or more diseases. Humans are more susceptible to these diseases with age, but dementia is not a normal or inevitable part of aging.

Dementia is defined as a severe loss of thinking, memory, and reasoning skills, such that a person's ability to carry out the normal activities of daily life is compromised or destroyed. These impairments result from the death of brain cells and neurons, and symptoms progress as the underlying disease kills ever-greater numbers of them. Dementia literally shrinks the brain. Patients eventually require a level of care that necessitates living in a nursing home or similar facility, and it is ultimately fatal.

The most common form of dementia (50 to 80 percent of cases) is Alzheimer's disease, followed by vascular dementia (some people have both of these diseases concurrently). The sixteen other causes of dementia collectively make up a much smaller percentage of cases.

A major precipitating cause of death for Alzheimer's patients is Alzheimer's-related pneumonia. Because of this, clients should include in their living wills whether they wish to receive antibiotics once they are seriously impaired.

There is no cure for dementia. There are medications approved for treatment that can slow the progression for months or years before the disease takes over, especially if these medications are started early in the process. Research continues in earnest, with promising antibodies and enzymes coming to the fore, especially those that prevent the sticky beta amyloid plaques that are a hallmark of Alzheimer's disease. Yet nothing can stop eventual progression or cure the disease.

The first signs of dementia may start manifesting ten or twelve years before diagnosable diminishment occurs. These signs may be vague and vary widely, but they include loss of memory of recent events, increased trouble judging distance, poor judgment, confusion, apathy, and difficulty doing everyday tasks properly.

Ten signs of progressing dementia include the following:

1. Memory loss that disrupts daily life, including misplacing things and being unable to retrace one's steps to find them. It is normal to forget names or appointments but remember them later.

2. Repeating the same question, story, or sentence in relatively brief periods, each time acting as if it were the first time. It is normal to tell the same story to multiple people and lose track of who already heard it, provided one is aware of the repetition.

3. New and increasing problems with words in speaking or in writing, especially noticeable inaccuracy in naming familiar objects, the inability to form and express a coherent thought, or trouble following a conversation. It is normal occasionally to be unable to find the proper word, but it is abnormal to be unable to converse.

4. Becoming lost in familiar places or along familiar routes and being unable to follow directions to find one's way.

5. Being unable to plan ahead, solve problems, make sound decisions, or handle complexity. It is normal to make mistakes sometimes, for example, in balancing a checkbook or forgetting to pack something when going on a trip. Likewise, missing an occasional monthly payment is normal, but being unable to manage a budget is not.

6. Difficulty completing familiar tasks: for example, giving wrong answers to simple addition or math problems, being unable to follow a recipe or play a familiar board game, or becoming confused about doing household tasks such as laundry.

7. Getting disoriented about day and date, color and contrast, people, places, and the passage of time. It is normal to get confused about which day or date it is, yet be able to figure it out.

8. A noticeable change in mood or personality, especially becoming more aggressive or agitated (although a person in later stages may become unusually gentle and compliant).

9. Neglecting personal hygiene, appearance, or nutrition, especially when normally these things were a priority.
10. Neglecting personal safety: for example, touching a hot pan or crossing a busy street without looking for traffic.

Early evaluation—as soon as symptoms manifest—is always to your clients' advantage. It is possible they don't have dementia and can be successfully treated. Even if they do have dementia, the diagnosis allows them to plan and make important decisions about care, transportation, living options, and financial and legal matters while they still can. It also allows them to get on medications to forestall the disease while researchers conduct trials that could find a cure. They may even be accepted into a clinical study and be able to take advantage of the latest technology and medication.

Your Office Protocol for Dementia

1. Educate your clients and accumulate resources before they need it.

It is not threatening to offer information on forgetfulness and dementia if it is clear that you offer it to every client and their family members. You can find an excellent, free twenty-four-page government booklet at http://www.nia.nih.gov/alzheimers/publication/understanding-memory-loss.

Although it is not specifically on dementia, another highly recommended book for your clients and their adult children is *Depression and Anxiety in Later Life: What Everyone Needs to Know* by Mark D. Miller and Charles F. Reynolds, III.

Check the bibliography in this book for more resources. In addition, watch for news reports on dementia research. Include bits of information on dementia when you send your newsletter or, if you don't send out a newsletter, put information in a folder to give to clients at meetings.

Accumulate a list of Alzheimer-related services in your area: clinics or doctors that specialize in the disease, support groups for family members, services that deliver meals, etc.

2. Secure advance permission to call others.

Ensure that every client signs a letter of diminishing abilities, which gives you express permission to call designated people and take action if you suspect any type of impairment. Clients may choose to have you call the same person designated as durable power of attorney for health care, or they may choose someone else.

Here is an example of such a letter:

I, (Client Name), give (professionals' names) of (firm name) permission to contact the person(s) listed below and my durable powers of attorney should they suspect a change in my physical, mental, or cognitive abilities..

Name to Contact: _____
Relationship: _____
Address: _____
Home Telephone: _____
Business Telephone: _____

Name to Contact: _____
Relationship: _____
Address: _____
Home Telephone: _____
Business Telephone: _____

Signed this ____ day of _____, 20__
Client Signature: _____
Witness or Notary Public: _____

When the letter is completed, keep a copy in the client's digital lockbox and in your files, and include it in your annual review to maintain accuracy, especially of contact information.

3. Ensure every client has all the relevant documents described in this reference guide.
It is especially necessary to have a durable power of attorney for health care and one for property. The durable power documents should include conditions, such as a formal diagnosis of dementia, that trigger their implementation. Review these documents every year for accuracy of content and beneficiaries.

4. Inform clients that you will incorporate some simple activities into every meeting.
Examples: Give clients a few coins and ask them to make change for a dollar. Ask them to list where they've been and what they've done since they got up that morning. Ask what day, time, and season it is. Ask them to describe in detail where they parked the car. Hold up familiar objects (screwdriver, pitcher, flower vase, key, glasses, etc.) and ask them to name the objects.

Always note and document the inability to correctly answer the above queries or any other signs such as the following:

» *Missing meetings frequently and uncharacteristically*
» *Undergoing personality changes, especially becoming more aggressive or angry*
» *Asking the same question repeatedly as if they had not asked it before*
» *Being confused about where they are or why they are there*
» *Engaging in any behavior or making any decision that causes you to raise an eyebrow or question the judgment behind it*

5. If you notice anything worrisome, talk with your client.

Here is an example:

"Helen, I told you a long time ago that I would be sure to bring it up to you if I saw any signs or symptoms that seem bothersome, and I'm fulfilling that promise. I noticed at our last two meetings that you asked the same question three times even though I answered it each time, and it took you an unusually long time to remember your son's name. It may be nothing, Helen. The cause may be one of several types of forgetfulness that are totally unrelated to dementia and are curable. Do you remember the booklet I gave you about this? It's entirely possible that you're having a reaction to a medication or that you have an infection. Maybe all that's wrong is a vitamin deficiency, or maybe there's another imbalance in your system that is throwing you off. I'd like you to be able to nip this in the bud if you can, especially before your family members or friends start accusing you of having dementia. Before it goes further, I think it would be a good idea to see your doctor and get it checked out. What do you say?"

Your client may respond angrily. If so, it suggests a greater likelihood that your concerns are valid, since increased aggression is a symptom of dementia. Additionally, people often express fear or embarrassment as anger, so if the client is experiencing doubts and fears, he or she may lash out at you.

Calmly repeat your assertion that there are many curable causes of temporary memory loss not caused by dementia, and you'd like her to be as healthy as possible so she can continue to live fully. You may also repeat that family members and friends are probably noticing these things as well and may begin to believe she has dementia even if it isn't true. Again, gently suggest she make a doctor's appointment.

If she agrees, volunteer to follow up by saying, "Good. Now, I don't mind following up next week to see whether you've been able to make an appointment or to find out what the doctor said. I care about your health and want to make sure you get what you need to live well and achieve your goals. I'll call on Tuesday to check in."

Document the details of your conversation, both in your own notes and in the post-meeting communication you send to your client.

6. Involve others.
If a client refuses to take action or delays going to a doctor, contact the people indicated in the diminishing abilities letter. Describe what you see and recommend that they get the client to a doctor for evaluation. If you have permission, talk with the spouse or adult children. Also, notify the people designated as durable powers of attorney.

Again, carefully document these conversations in your own notes and in written communications to the relevant parties.

7. Provide resources.
If a client is diagnosed with Alzheimer's, give the family another free booklet from the National Institutes of Health entitled *Caring for a Person with Alzheimer's Disease.* This is a substantial and comprehensive booklet. Get copies by calling 800-438-4380, or by ordering it or printing your own PDF at http://www.nia. nih.gov/alzheimers/publication/caring-person-alzheimers-disease.

Also, provide the list of resources for dementia patients that you previously developed so they can access services in the area.

8. Transition to working with the durable power of attorney.
After a diagnosis of dementia, include other family members and the designated durable power of attorney in all meetings. As long as possible, defer to your client for making final decisions while continually encouraging discussions with the "team." Keep your client in control as long as possible and gradually make the transition to others. Send notes and minutes from meetings plus summaries of every decision to all pertinent parties so everyone knows the process is transparent and you are acting responsibly.

Eventually, you will not be consulting the client at all, as the client loses capacity to make rational decisions or to clearly comprehend the complex factors involved.

When you follow these eight steps, you protect yourself and your clients during the entire process from suspicion of diminished capacity to diagnosis and beyond.

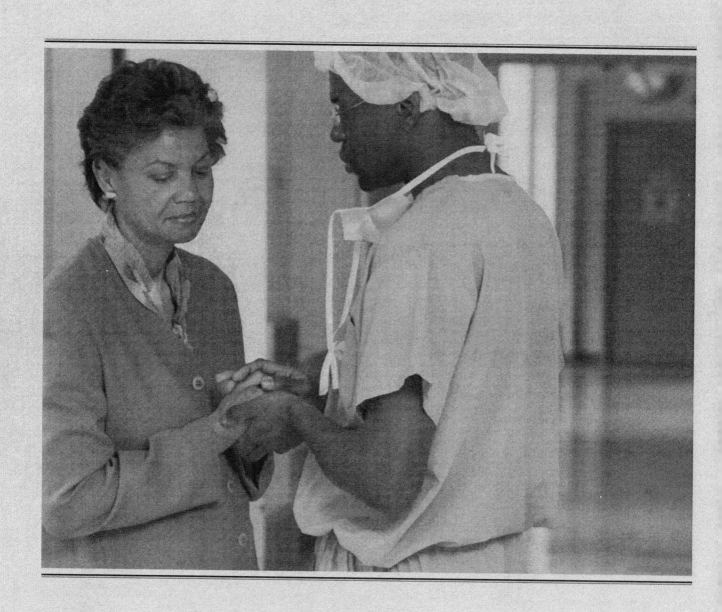

Clients with Terminal Illness

Background Information

Seventy percent of Americans die of a chronic or terminal illness, so it's likely that 70 percent of your clients will as well. You need to learn how to accompany them in financial and nonfinancial ways.

The family's grief process begins with the diagnosis. They vacillate between numbing shock and a raging river of emotions. It seems surreal and almost impossible to believe, especially if the diagnosis comes when the person is feeling reasonably healthy. The reality sinks in as treatments begin and the person's condition deteriorates.

Most people who hear of a diagnosis will try to cheer your ill clients on, regale them with stories of others who beat the odds, and urge them to fight. Strive to create a safe and confidential space where clients can also talk about their fears and face the practicalities of what could indeed happen before they wish it would. Incorporate the open-ended questions previously discussed in this book, review the list of phrases to avoid and the information on

anticipatory grief, and be willing to listen in ways that others don't.

In fact, be prepared to spend more than half the meeting talking about nonfinancial matters. Research with terminally ill people shows that thirty to sixty minutes of discussing their personal experience measurably decreases their levels of suffering and depression. In other words, they will leave your office feeling better in spite of the illness. Take the time to ask good questions and really listen before venturing into business.

Durable Powers

Recommend to ill clients that they meet with the person(s) designated as durable power of attorney for health care. With the known diagnosis and possible disease trajectory in mind, clients can explain more specifically what they want and when, including when they may want to stop treatments. You may wish to facilitate this discussion in your office; if not, follow up with clients until they arrange it themselves.

Recall that some investment custodians and banks require renewing or re-signing the paperwork for the durable power of attorney for property/finances on a regular basis. Ensure this task is completed as often as necessary as the disease progresses.

Suggest to clients that the person designated as durable power of attorney for property/finances be included in meetings so he or she is apprised of the finances and able to carry out the client's wishes.

Watch for Fatigue

People with serious or terminal illness, especially those undergoing chemotherapy, experience heightened levels of fatigue. Shorter, more frequent meetings are much better than long or complex appointments. Consider occasionally going to their house rather than having them come into the office. Prepare beforehand to set manageable agendas, get paperwork in order, and facilitate an efficient decision-making process.

When you do meet, frequently check in by asking questions: "Mike, we've been talking for an hour. What is your energy level right now, and what would you most like to do? We can stop for now and schedule another meeting in a few days or next week, or perhaps you have more energy today and would like to continue for a while. I'll adjust my schedule around your needs."

Concrete Help

When your client is dying, do not detach. Continue to send cards, make phone calls,

and support the client and his or her family. Consider taking concrete actions tailored to what you believe or know to be helpful. Here are a few ideas:

» Arrange for an afternoon of care so family caregivers can get a bit of respite to do whatever they wish
» Send a prepared meal once a week
» Give a subscription to a service such as Peapod that delivers groceries to the home
» Arrange for anything from a cake to a full-blown party if someone in the family has a birthday during the illness

Ensure that you stay engaged and involved so your clients know you will not abandon them as so many others have and will.

It is difficult for clients, especially those with a large network of friends, relatives, and acquaintances, to keep everyone else apprised of their treatment and progress without having to tell the same story fifty times. Suggest that the family set up a Caring Bridge site to eliminate this problem. (See http://www.caringbridge.org.)

This free service gives families a personal website to which their friends and family members can subscribe. The ill person posts updates as frequently as desired. Whenever there's a new post, all those on the subscription list receive an e-mail informing them that new information is available. They log onto the website, read the information posted there, and have the opportunity to respond with a message of their own.

This invaluable service streamlines the information process, disseminates updates immediately to everyone concerned, and facilitates dialogue and support.

If you wish, you can help clients set up their Caring Bridge site while they are in your office.

Four Things That Matter Most

In pivotal research with dying people, Dr. Ira Byock (a medical doctor and psychologist) found four things that dying people need to give and receive from the people they love. Those who are able to do so can die with greater peace and dignity, while their loved ones have fewer regrets and complications in their grief afterward. These four things bring a sense of completeness to the journey.

The four things are as follows:

The Four Things
That Matter Most

Thank you.
I forgive you.
I love you.
Goodbye.

1. "Thank you"

Life review, reflecting back on the decisions, mistakes, and joys that shaped life's trajectory, is an almost universal aspect of the dying process. Especially as people approach death, they search for reassurance that their life had meaning, made an impact, or touched someone. In the course of daily life, yelling at or complaining about family, coworkers, and friends is easier and more common than thanking or complimenting them. Dying people need to be thanked. In turn, they need to offer thanks to those who have been important to them.

2. "I forgive you"

We are not perfect people; we're just people. Dying patients know they have hurt others, and they have likewise been hurt. In fact, the easiest people to hurt are the ones most deeply loved. Yet they sometimes hold grudges so long they don't even remember why they got upset in the first place. Dying people usually realize that grudges and bitterness are no longer worth it. They need to ask for forgiveness for the wrongs they have done and to give forgiveness for the wrongs done to them. They need to forgive and be forgiven.

3. "I love you"

One of the greatest regrets survivors have is the failure to say "I love you" to the person who died. Sometimes, even if a couple loved each other very much, their last interaction was an argument, so the final words they exchanged were harsh, critical, or insulting. In other cases, a survivor had such a conflicted relationship that it was too difficult to voice those words before the person died. Regardless, mourners who do not or cannot express these words in some way cope with more complicated grief and more unfinished business as a result. Both dying people and those around them need to give and receive love.

4. "Goodbye"

When the time comes, everyone wants permission to go. People will sometimes hang on despite pain and suffering until they feel their loved ones will be OK and are ready to let them go. Saying goodbye does not make loved ones die; they are going to die anyway. It just gives them permission to do what they need to do with peace and grace. It can be as simple as saying, "I hope you can live for a long time yet, but if it's too much for you, if you can't do it anymore, then let go. It's OK. We will miss you and we will cry, but we will be all right. Go in peace."

Hospice

Hospice is an interdisciplinary team operating under a doctor's supervision to provide palliative care. Hospice has dual goals: helping patients live as fully as possible until they take their last breaths and facilitating a process where patients may die with dignity, grace, and peace. The hospice team can include nurses, social workers, psychologists, family members, and volunteers, depending on each patient's particular needs.

Palliative care treats the symptoms rather than trying to cure the underlying disease. It effectively controls pain levels, eases breathing, keeps lips and skin moist, and does everything possible to relieve the person's suffering. Hospice care tries to ensure no one dies in pain. Hospice workers also effectively accompany the dying person and the family. Their goal is to help the dying person achieve whatever he or she wishes before dying. They help people live the way they choose until the end.

Note that hospice isn't a place; it's a service. Most hospice care occurs in the dying person's home, although many hospitals, nursing homes, and independent facilities contain a hospice unit for people who can't go home or don't have others to care for them.

People must meet two criteria to qualify for insurance coverage of hospice care:

1. A prognosis from a doctor of less than six months to live AND
2. A commitment to forgo treatments aimed at a cure

In other words, your clients cannot go into hospice if they are still undergoing chemotherapy or any other curative treatment.

Because of this, too many people believe hospice is where you go when you've given up. That attitude keeps people from entering hospice until they are so close to death the organization cannot accomplish the good work it was created to do. Accepting the inevitable reality of death and making a concrete decision to live as fully as possible is a positive and strength-filled choice—quite the opposite of "giving up."

Likewise, hospice is not where people go when hope is gone. Hospice helps maintain the hopes of dying people even as those hopes change. For instance, at first the hope is for a cure. When that is impossible, a person may hope to live long enough to see a wedding or other occasion. If that is impossible (or after it is achieved), the patient may hope for reconciliation with someone or perhaps to see a certain person again. Hopes may change to the hope of staying at home, the hope of not being alone, or the hope for a peaceful death. Dying people always have hopes; those who care for them need to support the hopes they have rather than tell them what they should or should not hope for.

As you gather lists of resources for your clients, also collect information on the hospice organizations that operate in your area. Hospice organizations differ, so it's helpful to get detailed information about the specific services each one offers.

A highly recommended resource for your clients is the book *Final Gifts: Understanding the Special Awareness, Needs, and Communications of the Dying* by Maggie Callanan and Patricia Kelley. These two hospice nurses with decades of experience educate readers on the death process and on how to better understand the unique communications of dying people. Anyone facing the death of a loved one will learn invaluable information in its pages. The full reference is in the bibliography.

A Necessary Agenda

1. Build a team of experts if one isn't already in place. This team may include an accountant and/or tax lawyer, an estate-planning attorney, a medical-care planner, or anyone who can help provides services to the client and family. The important thing is that you are the hub of this wheel of services, coordinating the process.

2. Review investments. You may need to ensure there is enough liquid cash to pay for medical and other expenses. In addition, clients' goals change when they get a terminal diagnosis, and a restructuring may be in order.

3. Minimize estate taxes. Although you likely have been working on this aspect throughout your professional relationship, there may be additional things that you can do in light of the client's prognosis. For instance, the team members with expertise in this field may recommend that a couple give gifts or transfer assets to the dying spouse to get a stepped-up basis.

4. Review all beneficiaries. Examine every investment, annuity, will, and other document to ensure the beneficiaries are listed accurately and in accord with the client's current wishes.

5. Make an inventory of assets, ownership, and information necessary for probate. If you don't already have this information stored in your client's digital lockbox, see point #11 on page 76.

6. Assist your client in reviewing and updating the living will (including POLST or the Five Wishes form if he or she has one), the health-care proxy, the state's organ donor registry if the client wishes to donate organs, and the durable power of attorney for property/finances. Distribute copies to relevant parties.

The Possibility of a Family Meeting

Having a family meeting is an additional value-added step that you will likely consider only for your most valued clients because it's time consuming. There are several reasons to coordinate a family meeting despite the investment of time and resources.

» Research shows that adult children want to know their parents' wishes, desires, and wisdom.

» When parents can explain their legal, financial, and legacy decisions to the family while they're alive, you aren't in the position of having to explain after their death. It is more likely that they will direct any anger or disagreements at the parent instead of at you.

» You meet and connect with the next generation as you help create a profoundly meaningful experience for the entire family. They see you as a reliable resource person who provides comprehensive services extending beyond the financial realm. You distinguish yourself and your firm in their minds, and they come away with concrete reasons to refer you to their friends and associates.

Some professionals don't consider family meetings because of their fear of managing the family dynamics and potential blow-ups that could result. The advantage of suggesting it, though, is that clients will self-select. If they know their family is dysfunctional and the meeting would be a disaster, if tensions are too high, or if they simply don't feel comfortable, they'll opt out. Still, the mere fact that you offered will set you apart from other professionals.

Follow these fourteen steps to arrange and carry out the family meeting:

1. Ensure that your clients have completed and/or updated all financial, medical, and legacy documents. Encourage them to write a letter to the collective family or to each child. The letter can include aspects of the four things: thanks, forgiveness, love, and final messages. Clients can read this letter at the family meeting or seal it and give one to each family member.

2. Ask your clients for names, contact data, and a bit of information about each family member. Ask whether there are any "problem" people and what might be expected from them. Also, determine the identity of the "alpha child." This is the child to whom parents turn first and whom siblings recognize as the "leader." Usually the alpha child is a strong communicator, may already be actively involved in legacy planning, and will naturally step in if problems arise.

3. Send a note card to each adult member of the family. An example: "I am Amy Florian. I've had the privilege of serving your parents as their financial advisor for the past fourteen years. Your parents and I would like to arrange a meeting with the family to get everyone's legal and financial concerns on the table as you cope with your dad's diagnosis. I'll be in touch about setting up arrangements. In the meantime, please think about any issues or questions you'd like to discuss. I look forward to our meeting."

4. Invite the family to attend a meeting with a letter. Here's an example:

"Dear [name],

The [last name] family has been shaken by your dad's recent diagnosis. Issues you thought could be put off for another day now loom large. While I can't imagine what you're going through, it may seem like your entire world has been turned upside down. Your parents are amazing people and are among the very few of my clients with the wisdom and courage to bring the family together to talk about what is happening now and may happen in the future.

In a family gathering, which I'll facilitate at my office, your dad will offer personal messages to each of you, and everyone will have a chance to respond or add input. Then we'll cover various legal and financial documents, detailing his wishes for items ranging from medical treatment to eventual disposition of assets, and again you'll have a chance to respond or add input. During this process, you'll have your questions answered so you won't have to deal with surprises later, and there will be much less chance of guilt or second-guessing if you're required to make decisions on your dad's behalf.

It is important that everyone in the family be part of this meeting if possible. We sincerely hope you will participate, either by coming in to the office physically or by video conference call. I propose three alternatives for dates and times:

Please respond by Friday with your availability. In the meantime, know that although my contributions may be small, I'll do whatever I can to support you during this difficult time.

Sincerely,

[Professional's name]"

5. When you've set a date and time, invite any other professionals who can answer questions for the family. For instance, you may want a representative from hospice. Gather everyone at the appointed time, virtually or in person.

6. Begin the meeting by setting expectations: "Thank you all for your time. As I said in the invitation, our purpose here is let your dad

say what he wants to say his family, giving you the wisdom and life lessons he wants to pass on. Then we'll go over financial and legal instruments and answer your questions so there aren't any surprises along the way.

It's quite possible that not everyone will agree with all that we say here; that's OK. The point is to help everyone be aware of your dad's wishes, regardless of whether you agree with them, and to answer your questions. Throughout this process, we'll maintain an attitude of respect and allow each person to speak without judgment. I'll represent your mom and dad. If you have a disagreement that goes beyond the purview of this meeting, I'll do everything I can to help you resolve it yourselves. I may refer you, for instance, to a family counselor or to independent lawyers. Overall, though, try to remember that the end goal is to have everyone, regardless of whether you all agree, end up on the same page. Do you have any questions about the purpose and scope of the meeting?"

7. Allow for varying reactions: "Some or all of you may feel a wide range of emotions during this meeting. Some may show little outward emotion; others may cry. Some may want to talk about it; others may want to start taking actions to do something about it. Some may be hopeful; others may be sad. There may be laughter; there may be tears. It's all normal, and it's all OK. I've learned never to judge a person by the breadth and depth of their outward emotional reaction. Grief can be unpredictable, and it can make you feel like you're going crazy. You're not crazy; you're just grieving, and everyone does that differently."

8. If your client agreed to read messages to the family, invite it now. After the letters are read, invite family members to respond in whatever ways they wish.

If someone gets angry or walks out, note the appearance of issues that need to be faced. Offer to refer the person to a family counselor and say it is your sincere hope that he or she engages in the process and resolves things while there's still time. Hopefully, though, the client's wisdom and messages are well received, the children will have a chance to respond, and everyone will benefit.

9. Then proceed to the documents. For each one, allow the client to explain what he or she wants and then take questions. Begin with the durable power documents, and go on to organ donation, living will and/or POLST forms, wishes for funeral or services, comfort measures, and so forth. In particular, make sure your client explains the rationale behind choices for treatment or nontreatment so the entire family understands.

When you finish covering the other documents, turn to the last will and testament. Your clients don't have to disclose actual amounts, but they do need to explain in general what will happen after they die. Again, take questions. Then give family members a listing of all the information held in the digital lockbox (discussed in the chapter titled "Documents Every Client Should Have" on page 69) and invite them to call you when they need that information.

10. As you wrap up the meeting, recommend or give to each person the book *Final Gifts: Understanding the Special Awareness, Needs, and Communications of the Dying* (see the bibliography chapter for the reference). Tell them you recommend this book to everyone when they are still healthy because of the invaluable information it holds.

11. Summarize what just happened: your client was able to give messages to the family, the family members found out about the documents and the client's wishes so they

could more confidently make decisions without second-guessing, and they received important information about what we all will inevitably face.

12. End with something like this: "The message I most hope you take from this meeting is that financial planning, advance directives, wills, legacy writings, and other documents are things every person should be doing all along. Let the shock of your dad's diagnosis help you do these things now and then keep them updated. After all, none of us knows how long we have. How can you make it easier on the people you love if something happens to you? What do you need to know about others you love in case something happens to them? What can we all do right now to live better so if we die tonight, or if someone we love dies tonight, there are no regrets? As much as possible, use the lessons of this diagnosis to help you live better until the day you take your last breath." Then invite them to contact you any time they have questions and thank them for their participation.

13. Give everyone a warm handshake. Some may reach out for a hug; others will shake your hand and walk away.

14. The next day, mail a note to all family members and include your e-mail address. Ask for feedback—anything they appreciated about the meeting and one thing they wish had been different. Thank them again for their time and tell them you're always willing to answer their questions or serve them in any way you can.

Although you will not conduct these family meetings for every client, it can be an educational and meaningful experience. It connects you to the next generation, establishes your expertise, and increases the chances you will serve more of the family members.

Statistics and Stories to Demonstrate Knowledge and Raise the Topic of Planning

One of the most daunting tasks in advance planning is raising the topic with clients in the first place. In our death-denying society, professionals and clients alike would rather avoid it altogether. As you become more comfortable talking with clients about these issues, you realize that facing the inevitability of death will not kill you. Quite to the contrary, acknowledging the reality of disability, aging, diminishment, loss, and death can help people live more fully and with greater appreciation, awareness, and joy.

In addition, if you protect your clients in every aspect of their lives, their gratitude when those tough times arise offers you the satisfaction of knowing you truly served their needs, which positions you for client loyalty and referrals. Preparing and protecting your clients in financial and nonfinancial ways is good for everyone—and good for business. This chapter provides information and skills that will help you address these difficult topics in the office.

A Few Principles to Incorporate

Your clients don't consider themselves "typical." Use this to your advantage to introduce the topic of planning for the inevitable. For instance, you can say, "Not everyone has the courage and understanding to complete all these documents. You're in the upper tiers of people in the country if you do. And at the same time, you remain in greater control of your life, you protect your family, and you make your own decisions even if you're temporarily incapacitated and unable to speak for yourself."

Since your clients don't want to think about dying (nor do they truly believe they are going to die), frame your discussions in positive terms. Instead of saying, "The goal is to help you have what you want even when you're dying," say, "The goal is to help you live as fully as possible until you take your last breath." Speak to them in terms of living fully, living the way they choose right up until the end, making the most of every day of life, and the like.

Another helpful introduction: "Chances are excellent that dementia or serious illness is a long way off, if it ever happens to you at all. Still, I can help you put some documents in place that will keep you in control of your life and your medical treatment, no matter what occurs or when. At the same time, you take the burden of decision-making off the shoulders of your family members. You take away their second-guessing, arguing, and feeling guilty because you've made sure they know what you want."

Statistics That Reinforce the Topic

These six statistics might grab the attention of clients, especially if you combine them with the accompanying invitational question:

1. Ninety percent of people prefer to die in their own homes, but only fifteen percent do.

   Where do want to live the last days of your life? Let's get that in writing to increase the chances you will beat the statistics and live your final time where you want.

2. Over 70 percent of deaths in the United States are "negotiated" in some way— someone has to make a decision about treatment or withdrawal of treatment. Yet, most people never write down what they want for themselves, and only 38 percent of people who do write it down ever give that information to anyone else, including their doctor.

   Isn't that crazy? The average person doesn't let people know what he or she wants for medical treatment or give the information to the people who need to have it! You can do better than that. In fact, I have a document here that provides an easy way to start thinking about some treatments you want or don't want in different situations, so you make your own decisions instead of being at the mercy of someone else's judgments. Let's also make sure you legally appoint the person you trust to carry out your wishes if you're in surgery, in a

coma, or in any other condition that prevents you from speaking for yourself. I'd like you to retain as much control as possible. Is that what you want?

3. In the United States, 2,600 people die unexpectedly every day, and an American dies in a car accident every twelve minutes.

   Suppose you had died in a car accident on the way home yesterday. Today, would your family know what to do and where all your information is located? If we complete these documents, the people you love will have all the information they need, and the nice side benefit is that they can carry out your wishes even though you are not there to state them.

4. I bet you and your family members are like every person in the country in one respect: you want to retain your mental faculties throughout your life. But the reality in the United States is that 5.4 million people over sixty-five—one in every eight Americans in that age group—have Alzheimer's disease, nearly half of people age eighty-five and older have Alzheimer's, and another person in America develops Alzheimer's every sixty-nine seconds. We currently have medications that can slow the progress of the disease if it's caught early, buying time for more research to be done. There are also several types of forgetfulness that are not caused by dementia, and most of the time they are treatable and curable.

   Let's handle this from several aspects. First, I ask all my clients to sign a diminishing capacity letter, giving me permission to call the people of your choice if your own capacity seems to be diminishing. Second, you want to know what to look for in your family members. I have a booklet here that explains the most troublesome signs of potential dementia; it also explains the curable non-dementia causes of forgetfulness. Let's look at the booklet together, and I'll give you a copy to take home. Then, if you ever notice a memory problem in your family, we can get it checked out. It may not be Alzheimer's, and perhaps the problem can be easily cured. On the other hand, if dementia is beginning, we may be able to get treatment right away and keep it from progressing unchecked.

5. If people are given a choice whether their kids could inherit money and material possessions OR their wisdom and life lessons, they overwhelmingly choose the wisdom and life lessons. Interestingly, the adult kids do too. In fact, it's rather dramatic—77 percent feel it's very important to pass on their values and life lessons, 34 percent consider it very important to pass on possessions that have emotional or sentimental value, and only 10 percent felt it was very important to pass on financial assets.

   How do you want people to remember you? If you had dropped of a heart attack yesterday, what would you wish you could say to your loved ones today? What do you want your kids and grandkids to learn from you? We focus a lot in our meetings about leaving a financial legacy, ensuring financial security, and passing on your money, but that's just the tip of the iceberg. I can help you in nonfinancial ways to pass a legacy on to your survivors that is more important than just money, so your spirit can continue to live on in the next generations.

6. A major study said that most people want a "dignified death."

   What does "dignified death" mean to you? I can provide the necessary paperwork to help ensure you have the dignity you want even at the end of your life, whether that happens next week or many, many years from now.

Stories that reinforce the topic

Not everyone is interested in statistics. Many people are captivated more by stories and emotional factors. These eight examples vary depending on the referenced document. The examples are all factual (it's always more effective to use true stories). You may employ these and/or build your own repertoire from news reports, books, your client or family experiences, and other sources.

1. Tim was a thirty-six-year-old father of three when he was in a construction accident that caused second- and third-degree burns over 93 percent of his body. He had less than a 1 percent chance of survival and was in an induced coma for four months. Against all odds, he survived and is still alive twelve years later.

   If you were in an accident and in an induced coma for months, who would you want making decisions such as whether to hook you up to certain machines or whether to perform a particular surgery? Are you confident the person you named knows what you want and would do what you want? Would you like me to explain your options, coordinate the process of informing that person, and help ensure your wishes are followed even when you can't speak for yourself?

2. You may remember Terri Schiavo, who went into a persistent vegetative state after an accident when she was only twenty-six years old. She never told anyone what kind of treatment she wanted or how she wanted to live out her life if she were in that condition. (After all, she was only twenty-six, and things like that don't happen to young people, right?)

   Fifteen years later, she remained in a persistent vegetative state, and her family was still fighting about it. The fighting rose to such a level of intensity that they went to court to wrest control from each other. For the following four years, the national news showed videos of Terri in a seriously diminished state. The state government and eventually the U.S. government got involved. In the process, a very private and personal story appeared on a very public stage. Ultimately, Terri's feeding tube was removed and she died in 2005, with the autopsy showing she had no cognitive brain function left.

Do you want a potential illness of yours to risk dividing your family, putting hospital videos of you on television, and ultimately leaving decisions on your care up to the courts or the government? Would you like to talk about it together so I can help you fill out the documents that let you make those decisions yourself regardless of your health status?

3. I recently attended a funeral where the son got up and read the most beautiful eulogy to his dad, talking about how much he appreciated him and how much the family would miss him. There wasn't a dry eye in the place.

How do you want people to remember you? What is more important to you—that you pass on your money to your kids and grandkids or that they know the wisdom and life lessons you'd like to pass on? Did you know there are ways to make that happen, and I can help you with it?

4. Amy's husband died in a car accident when he was twenty-five. They talked on the phone forty-five minutes before the accident happened, and the last thing they said to each other was "I love you." Denise's husband dropped dead of a heart attack. They loved each other very much, but they'd had an argument and their last words to each other were angry and unkind.

If the unthinkable happened and a drunken driver slams into your car on the way home today, are there things you wish you could say to people you love? Would you like to hear about ways you can ensure your last words are heard even if you don't have the chance to say them in person?

5. Are you aware of what happened after Jimi Hendrix died? Because he hadn't completed a formal will, instead of his money going to the brother Jimi loved, it went to the father who abandoned the family when Jimi was young, who didn't raise him, and who ended up passing it on to a half-sister that Jimi barely knew. Likewise, Heath Ledger did not update his will after his daughter was born. When he died after the Batman movie, all his money went his dad and none to his little girl.

We've done a lot of planning and investing, and you have a valuable portfolio. Would you like me to help put your wishes into writing or update and revise them so you control your legacy? Can we look at the beneficiaries on all your investments, insurance, and legal documents to make sure they're up-to-date?

6. At the age of forty, Richard crashed his bicycle on a beautiful fall day. He spent two days in the intensive care unit but died from massive head and internal injuries. Richard was an organ donor. His heart went to a fifty-five-year-old husband and father of three. Doctors transplanted his liver into a forty-nine-year-old married man with four children and two grandchildren. One kidney went to an eleven-year-old boy who was able to end his dialysis treatments, and the other kidney went to a forty-three-year-old mother. Richard's wife Karen finds meaning and comfort that Richard's legacy literally lives on in the world and that his organs are helping four other families.

On the other hand, Kelly and John chose not to donate their young daughter's organs when she died, and Keith's faith tradition does not allow organ donation. It is an individual decision, and one that deserves to be respected.

If you were to die suddenly, would you find meaning in donating your organs, or would you prefer not to do so? Regardless of which you choose, would you like me to help you make your wishes as legally binding as possible so others can't override them?

7. Tara and Mike got married when they were twenty-four. Both worked until two years later when the first of their three kids was born. At the time, they decided they would live on Mike's income so Tara could stay home. When they were thirty-two, they were standing in the kitchen cooking dinner together when Mike dropped dead of an undiagnosed congenital heart condition. They hadn't bought any life insurance because they felt it was too complicated and they'd have plenty of time before they needed it. Within three weeks after Mike's death, Tara had to find childcare for their three young kids and find a full-time job for herself, even though she'd been out of the workforce for six years.

There is one main reason that people buy life insurance: they have someone they love for whom they also feel financial responsibility. Who fits that description in your life? Would you like to make sure you have enough of the right kinds of coverage so you know you won't be responsible for a nightmare situation like this one? I can explain the options to you, and we can set things up so you know your family won't have to scramble for money if something happens to you.

8. Ray was diagnosed with Alzheimer's disease. He decided that once he reached a level where he could no longer care for himself, dress himself, and carry on a coherent conversation with loved ones he recognized, he didn't want any further medical interventions. If his heart stopped, he didn't want resuscitation. If he contracted pneumonia, he wanted to die of the pneumonia rather than receive antibiotics. He didn't want a feeding tube. He explained his wishes to his family, completed all the legal documents including a new document that became his doctor's standing order, and chose a health-care proxy he could trust to carry out his desires. Ray eventually had to move into a nursing home. His wife was holding his hand as he napped one day when he suddenly went into cardiac arrest. She knew his wishes and continued to simply hold his hand, stroke his face, and tell him goodbye. He died peacefully with her by his side.

What would you want if you were in Ray's situation? If you are ever diagnosed with dementia, is there a point at which you would no longer want life-extending intervention, or would you want every available technology to be used? Would you like some education on the documentation you can complete to make your wishes as legally binding and enforceable as possible, so you get to live the way you want until your last breath?

These types of stories and statistics should help you get the conversation started with your clients. Then rely on the documents themselves to guide you. Work with an attorney on all legal documents, but remember to position yourself as the quarterback or the hub of the wheel, coordinating everything for your client's benefit.

Value of Role-Play

Your ultimate goal is to create a unique, personal, holistic experience for your clients. Mistakes matter, but genuine support matters more.

Yet how do you avoid mistakes? Despite what you've learned, the next time you walk into the services and extend your hand to greet a grieving client, the first words out of your mouth are probably going to be "I'm so sorry." These habits are so deeply ingrained that it takes conscious effort to change them.

The only way to embrace these skills and make them as habitual as "I'm so sorry" is to engage in regular role-play in your office. Consider setting aside fifteen minutes a week to act out various scenarios. Your administrative assistant can answer a call from a "grieving client" one week. The next week, imagine you are at the services or in the first appointment after the services. This regular practice keeps your skills sharp and retrains your brain. Then, whether it's a phone call, office visit, visitation, funeral, or any other situation, you and your staff will be prepared, and your clients will benefit.

Role-playing is not a waste of time. It is an investment of time—one that promises to pay off in sustainable and measurable ways for your business.

Compensation

Some professionals, especially those who operate solely on commission, are understandably concerned about the amount of time required to implement the skills in this guidebook. You have to decide for yourself how to structure compensation for these invaluable services, recalling that when you bring value to your clients, especially value they aren't receiving elsewhere, it is worth paying for.

You may wish to fund some of these high-reward activities with your marketing budget. A good question to ask yourself is how much time, energy, and money you spend on getting a single new client. Then consider how much time, energy, and money you're willing to spend to keep the clients you already have, deepen these relationships immeasurably, and increase the chances you'll be able to bring their family, friends, and associates into the firm as well. Walking people through the toughest times of their lives may be the best marketing strategy you can employ.

Regardless, your compensation structures and the level of priority you place on implementing these skills confirm the fabric of your business model going forward. This deserves strategic consideration. Already, some of the most successful firms in the country are outsourcing many aspects of investment management to allow for increased time on client relationships. They recognize that firms can no longer distinguish themselves by providing wise financial advice. Too many other firms offer the same. Transaction-based business will not be sufficient for long. The wave of the future lies in skills such as you find in this book.

Consider, then, your business going forward. Create compensation structures that fit your firm's values and your firm's value proposition. Decide how deeply to integrate these skills and practices in order to accomplish your goals, and build in proper payment for your efforts.

When Your Pen Hovers Over the Page: Condolence Cards and When to Send Them

General Information and Schedule

Professional firms make it a practice to send condolence cards when clients experience a death in the family. Too many don't know what to write, and they stop after one card. In this section, you learn how to make an ongoing difference in your clients' lives.

Depending on the client and the situation, you may wish to send something at the following times:

» Two to three days after the services
» Three to four weeks after the services OR after the first office appointment
» On some of the monthly anniversaries of death
» On special days like birthdays (including the birthday of the person who died), wedding anniversaries, graduations, holidays, Valentine's Day, or any other important occasions
» On the anniversary of death for several years afterward

From this spectrum, choose the frequency and cost of contact based on the nature and value of a client's relationship with you and your firm.

Gifts you may want to include:
» Gift certificates for a dinner delivered to the home, a restaurant meal, coffee, a movie, a massage or day spa, or anything else you believe will be relaxing or comforting
» A tapestry made from the deceased person's portrait (e.g., PhotoWeavers.com)
» A small plant, especially if the client would put it into a garden
» A book on grief, preferably one closely matched to the client's situation (see the bibliography in this book for suggestions)
» Notice of your donation in memory of the person who died
» A tree planted in memory of the person who died
» Some truly homemade foods if you or someone in your office likes to bake
» A shredding service for papers the client needs to clear out
» A single flower in a bud vase

» A monthly fruit or food basket delivery
» Whatever you believe your client will enjoy

Carefully consider the bereavement card you choose, especially for the first card or two. Choose a text that is authentic and honest rather than one that denies the death or minimizes the loss. For instance, avoid texts that assert the person hasn't really died but is simply in the next room or texts that instruct mourners not to cry because their loved one is happy. Ensure that any prewritten text meets the criteria for grief support already discussed in this guide.

Later cards may have an inspirational verse or simply an attractive picture and may have few or no words inside.

Regardless of the text on the card, be sure to include personalized, handwritten comments. Clients know it's all too common for an administrative assistant to buy a card, sign it for the boss, and send it. Your clients need to know you took the time and care to write something personal.

In the first card, you may wish to reference the services—the lovely music, the moving eulogy, or the number of people who turned out to show their support. In every card, remember to write the name of the person who died, and always keep the focus on the survivors, not on you.

The following pages contain a wealth of ideas on which to base your card texts, divided into categories for a variety of situations and timings. Use these as written, or adapt them so they sound like you and more closely fit your client's circumstances. These texts also contribute ideas you can add to your repertoire when talking with clients in the office or in other venues.

Texts of cards

Immediately After a Death

When I learned of the sudden death of your beloved [name], my heart instantly went out to you. What words could I possibly say that could comfort you at this time? There are none. So I join my tears with yours as I remember [name's] life and what [he/she] meant to so many.

When a loved one dies long before [his/her] time, it turns everything upside down. Any answers to the question "Why?" ring hollow. As you navigate this heart-wrenching time, know that you are in my thoughts [and prayers]. Every day I take a moment to let your grief remind me of what is most important in life and, in so doing, I honor the life of [name].

Though I share your sadness, I cannot enter into the depth of your grief. All I can do today is use a few minutes to honor [name's] memory by deliberately extending a kindness to another person in memory of [his/her] life. I promise that today somebody will smile because [name] lived.

[Name's] death shocked me to the core. I could not believe it. Yet if it shocked me, how much more devastated you must be! I cannot imagine your pain, nor can I bring [name] back. What I can do is assure you of my support and offer to help you remember the wonder that was your [husband/child/other relationship]. I'll call you soon to get together for coffee.

If the number of people who attended services provided a measure of success, then [name] was more than successful. Yet, [name] didn't measure success by the number of people who loved [him/her]. Rather, [he/she] measured it by how often [he/she] could lend a hand and share [his/her] skill at [_____] with the people [he/she] served so well. Along with so many others, I join you in gratitude for [his/her] life and sadness for [his/her] death.

Does one life make a difference? [Name]'s did. Though [he/she] was known and loved by many (as evidenced by the outpouring of people for the services), I think it was the depth of [his/her] commitment to the well-being of [his/her] friends that touched me most during the time I knew [name]. That is a memory I will cherish for the rest of my life.

[Name] was a gem—one of the finest [women/men] I've ever known. In fact, I will always remember the time when . . . [story]. I know that memories like this cannot erase the pain of loss, but perhaps as you allow yourself to cry and grieve, you can also allow yourself sustaining moments of laughter and joy. As you walk this journey, I will do whatever I can to make things easier for you and to honor [name]'s life.

[Name] was an interesting and colorful character. Everyone knew [he/she] could be as ornery as a stubborn mule, and [he/she] certainly had issues. Yet you saw the heart beneath the outside layers. You were devoted to [him/her] and cared for [him/her], and I imagine [he/she] loved you more than [he/she] had the capacity to express. Your lives intertwined in so many ways that it is impossible for anyone else to know the depth of your loss. In the midst of this complex situation, I will do my best to help you honor [name]'s life and to support you as you move into a future without [his/her] presence at your side.

[Name]'s death was not a surprise, and it would be normal if you felt some relief that [he/she] is no longer suffering. Yet I know it is still intensely painful to lose your life companion of so many years. Every waking moment is different for you now, and it will take a long time to build a new sense of normalcy in your life. I want you to know that I will be here for you throughout this process to support you in whatever ways I can.

It is difficult to measure the "success" of a life. Yet, when I look back on [name's] life, it is impossible to see it as anything other than incredibly successful. Why? Because [name] left [his/her] little part of the world a better place. Nothing more can be asked of anyone, and [name] answered that call in [her/his] own unique way. I am better for having known [name]. You are in my thoughts and prayers as you struggle through these first months without [name] by your side.

Kahlil Gibran wrote, "When you are sorrowful, look into your heart and you shall see that you are weeping for that which has been your delight." [Name] was truly your delight. I am thinking of you.

I didn't know [name] well, nor did you and I have occasion to speak of [him/her] often over the years. However, in the few times that [name's] came up or when I saw you together, it was obvious that you loved, admired, and respected [him/her]. I hope the memory of your treasured relationship with [name] helps sustain you even in the sadness of grief.

Helen Keller said, "All that we love deeply becomes a part of us." [Name] has died, and there is no way to take away that reality or its implications. At the same time, you are a different person because [he/she] loved you, and no one can ever take that away from you. As long as you live, a part of [him/her] lives on in you. I hope that knowledge gives you courage in your darkest times.

I didn't know [name] beyond our casual relationship. However, I was always impressed with how much [he/she] cared for you and the family and tried to do what was best for those [he/she] loved. As you cope with [name]'s death, I will honor [his/her] commitment to your well-being by offering a listening ear, a willing shoulder, and on occasion, a good dinner out.

There is no way to adequately honor the memory of [name] or the difference [he/she] made to so many, including me. Yet I want to try. So today, I am donating to [organization or foundation the person or family supported or organization that funds research on the cause of the death] in [his/her] name. In this way, many people will continue to benefit, and [name]'s legacy will live on.

All of us here at the office have been affected by [name]'s death. We are donating to [the organization the family requested in lieu of flowers], and we know that as our donation joins with those of so many others, the world will be a better place because [name] lived. Our support won't stop there, though. We will continue to do everything we can in this difficult time to support you and help you move forward as [name] wanted.

This is a time of mixed emotions. It is, of course, a relief to you that [name] is not suffering any-more and a relief that you don't have to stand by helplessly watching [him/her] suffer. Yet you miss [him/her] desperately, and wish [he/she] were still alive. Both sides of the equation are normal, even though you may feel like a ping-pong ball going back and forth between them. Do your best to honor your emotions and allow them to surface whenever they come. I will do what I can to walk with you through this difficult process and help you regain your life.

Tears are not a bad thing. They contain chemicals that help relieve stress, they help us heal, and they give expression to the pounding ache inside. The tears will eventually stop, and peace will come. In the meantime, though, I hope you find the strength to let them spill out and join the tears of so many people who mourn [name]. We have lost a treasure, and it is fitting that our tears rain on a world that will never be the same. My sorrow joins with yours, and my thoughts [and prayers] are with you.

You and [name] have been my friends for so long that my heart breaks with you over [his/her] death. I know I can't enter all that you feel or take away your pain. What I can do, though, is offer the strength that comes from my caring about you. On this lonely journey, know that you are not alone and that I walk with you.

Few people receive the gift of being loved without measure, but I know you were. In fact, the depth of your grief now is an indication of the depth of the love you shared with [name]. Though life will never be the same, may the knowledge of so great a gift help you get through the pain.

When my [relationship] died, it was as if I'd lost half of my body. There were days when the memories of [name] would make it better and days when they made it worse. Did I hate the pain? Yes. Yet eventually, I learned not to fear it because it was also a manifestation of the love we had. I don't know whether you feel the same way as I did, but I am here to help you work through the pain, minimize the fear, and remember the love.

It is said that spouses who are married for a long time start to look and act like each other. If that is the case, then you are doubly blessed because [name] was a beautiful person inside and out. [He/she] seemed to bring a sense of peace and serenity wherever [he/she] went, and I certainly experienced that during the times we met. While life is anything but serene for you right now, I wanted you to know the impact [name] had on my life. I am grateful for the gift of having known [him/her].

[Name] was an extraordinary person, one of those whom no one can ever replace. Know that my thoughts are with you as you happily recall your years together and yet cry through the heartache [his/her] absence brings.

Some lives are measured by how many people called them "friend." Other lives are measured by the incredible impact they had on a few. Though I only know the story of [name's] life, from what you have told me, [he/she] was a person of unassuming generosity who had a long-lasting impact on the lives of those who knew [him/her] best. That is a legacy worth celebrating with both smiles and tears. I share both with you.

When we lose a trinket, we mourn only momentarily, and then life goes on as before. When we lose a treasure, nothing is the same and the void is deep. You have lost a treasure. So have we. We are thinking of you.

It was amazing to see the number of people overflowing the services last week. It has to be gratifying to know that [name] touched so many lives and that you aren't the only one who thought [he/she] was a true gem. I hope that over the next couple of weeks you get to read the letters and cards written by those who care and know what a special gift you had, even as you realize what a loss [his/her] death brings. I am remembering with you, and I will do whatever I can to help make this difficult process a little smoother and easier for you.

[Name]'s death has affected me deeply. I can't imagine what it's like for you, who were so much closer to [him/her] than I. You are losing a best friend, a trusted companion, an unending source of wisdom, a sounding board, a helpful mentor, and so much more. The struggle will continue for a long time to come. It is hard to let go of one so loved, yet that love will forever remain a part of us. I know we will continue to share stories and memories as you move into the future without [his/her] physical presence by your side.

Grief accompanies a long illness, and you have known its ways already as you watched [name] slowly die. The two of you gleaned deep lessons as you battled [his/her] illness for so long. Even as you mourn [his/her] absence, perhaps those lessons and the strength [he/she] showed then can help you move forward and live more fully now. Know that I am here to help you do that.

I never knew your [relationship] and so I cannot do what I'd most like to do . . . offer a happy remembrance of how [he/she] touched my life. Yet I can offer my listening ear and would love to learn more about [name]. I will call to see if you are available for [a slice of pie and coffee] sometime in the next few weeks.

Seasons continually change, chapters end and others begin, and yet life and love know no reason to die. Though [name]'s physical absence leaves a gaping void, [he/she] lives on in our hearts, and we carry [him/her] forward in our lives. I am here to help you honor [name] by listening to the stories of the past, even while you build new stories for a future enriched by [his/her] memory.

Certain people come into our lives and touch us deeply. I know [name] touched so many with [his/her] amazing ability to persevere through the challenges of having a disability. What an inspiration [name] was to others with [her/her] attitude toward life! [He/she] inspired me too, and our firm is donating to [name of foundation or organization that supports people with that disability]. You've lost an incredible companion, yet the world is a better place because [he/she] lived.

Charles Dickens wrote, "And can it be that in a world so full and busy, the loss of one creature makes a void in any heart so wide and deep that nothing but the width and depth of eternity can fill it up!" The death of [name] leaves that kind of a void. You are in my thoughts and prayers.

I have rarely heard such touching eulogies as I heard at [name]'s services. I was inspired to live my own life more fully in [his/her] honor.

As you move forward, I will do whatever I can, personally and professionally, to help you do the same.

At the services, I told you one of the memories of [name] that I will carry with me forever. [Reminder of the story]. Lately, I was also remembering [give another memory or story]. I'm sure that as time goes by, there will be many more stories and memories rising up. [Name] will be missed in so many ways. Through it all, I am here for you to help you live in a way that honors your memories.

It's been two weeks now since the funeral. I imagine extended family members have left, and people around you are getting back to their "normal" lives. I know your grief will last longer than a few weeks, and I will continue to be here for you as we go forward.

Acknowledgment of a Recent or Upcoming Appointment

It hasn't been long since [name]'s death, yet you've had to handle so many details and do so much paperwork. It has to seem overwhelming at times, and I will continue to help you in whatever ways I can. As each piece falls into place, you are moving into a future that will be very different than you had planned but one that can still hold joy and peace.

Thank you for making the time to meet with me this week. I know it's hard to look at portfolios and make decisions without [name]. Yet I think we got a good start, and I will be here to help guide you. My goal, as always, is to help you live the way you wish and to reach your goals, even as they change in this time of transition. Together, we will maintain [name]'s legacy and protect your financial future.

Has it really been [time] since [name] died? I look forward to our appointment next week so I can catch up on what is happening for you right now. I will always do everything I can personally and professionally to support you and help make this difficult time a little bit easier.

You made some good decisions this week in our meeting. Yet I know that when we cover so much at once, you may realize you have questions you didn't think of when you were in my office. I want to make sure we address your concerns, so I will call you every Tuesday morning for the next couple of weeks. My purpose is just to check in and see what questions you may have. It's good to know we're working together in ways that honor [name] and provide solid protection for you. I look forward to continuing the conversation.

After a loved one's death, some people don't even want to think about financial or legal matters while others are so worried about them they can think of little else. Both are normal. Wherever you stand on the continuum, I look forward to our upcoming appointment so I can make sure I am on the same page with you. I am committed to providing wise guidance that helps you make good decisions at the appropriate times, not rushing you into anything, and providing full information so you can make the best decisions for yourself. I'll see you on [day] at [time].

Have you had countless people telling you what you "should" do and what decisions you "should" make? I look forward to our appointment so we can sort through all the well-meaning advice to determine where true wisdom lies in your situation. Bring all your questions and concerns. I will help you examine the options, look objectively at pros and cons, and make decisions that you feel are best for you. I look forward to seeing you on [day] at [time].

In our meeting this week, it was obvious you have many people who care about you. That is a wonderful thing until they start telling you how to act, decide, and live your life. As I told you in the office, I will take care to honor their good-hearted recommendations as we examine them together to determine whether they shape a good path for your future. I will call you on Thursday morning to see whether you have follow-up questions from our meeting and to help ensure we continue working seamlessly together to protect you and honor [name]'s legacy. I'll be in touch.

Monthly or Yearly Anniversary of a Death

It's hard to believe that over six months have passed since your [relative] died. Time takes on a different dimension when we lose someone we love, as if it were simultaneously a long time and just a moment ago when [he/she] was just a phone call or an arm's length away. I want you to know I'm thinking of you today.

You're probably finding by now that most people are afraid to mention [name]'s name. In fact, they will talk about anything and everything except [him/her]. They mean well. They're just afraid they will upset you or make your grief worse. They don't understand that you want and need to talk about [him/her] and remember, even if tears come in the process. Despite the reluctance of so many, I hope you find opportunities to speak [his/her] name and tell the story. Know that I will always listen and honor your memories.

I'm still trying to comprehend that [name] died. I guess nothing ever prepares you to receive news like that. Do you remember at the visitation when I told you I will always remember [name]'s [smile, laugh, caring heart, or other characteristic]? I shared that story with a mutual friend who heartily agreed. Nothing will ever replace [name]'s [characteristic], and we will carry that memory with us forever.

It has been long enough now since [name] died that you know with certainty nothing can take away the pain. Still, I hope you can at least enjoy [a cup of your favorite coffee, a massage, a good meal that you don't have to cook, etc.] with the enclosed gift card.

Your life is so dramatically different than it was [number] months ago. You have borne incredible pain, yet you have shown gritty determination. Each month that passes brings you closer to healing, closer to laughing freely, and closer to putting pieces of your life into place. It is an honor to call you my friend, and today I wanted to let you know how much I care.

It was delightful to see you smile when we got together last week. I know grief and loneliness are still present, yet I see hope and happiness beginning to peek through. Gradually the sad times will become less frequent and less intense, and happy times will become more frequent and more intense. You create a wonderful testimony to [his/her] love by allowing yourself to live fully enriched by [his/her] memory. Today, I remember and smile with you.

Keep in mind that there will always be people who expect you to grieve in the way they believe you "should." If you don't, they may be genuinely concerned for you and/or think something's wrong with you. Be assured, though, that there is nothing wrong with you. What you're experiencing is normal for a grieving person. Follow your own path, and know that understanding people can be there with you wherever you are. I hope you'll allow me be one of them.

Sometimes it seems like forever since [name] died, and yet it seems like yesterday. It can seem like healing will never come, and yet you've come so far already. As you negotiate your way through this crazy sense of time, know that I am by your side. I'll call soon.

It's been about [number] months since [name] died. I wonder if you feel like you're on a roller coaster ride at times—some days feeling up and other days feeling down, as if you're right back where you were when you learned of [name's] death. It can make you feel like you're going crazy, but you're not. This is normal for grieving people. Whether you are "up" or "down," know that you are healing slowly but surely. Remember often, cry when you feel like it, and welcome the moments of joy that sustain you.

You're probably tired of people telling you how strong you are. I imagine that sometimes you want to tell them you feel like a strand of blown glass ready to break with the slightest wind. You want to tell them that you put on your "public face" when you go out, but it's a different story when you walk back into your empty house. You want to tell them to change places with you for a while and then tell you how strong you are. They just don't understand. So let such comments slide off and clatter to the ground. Then keep putting one foot in front of the other. Every morning that you wake up and get out of bed is one more morning toward healing. Life can be good again, but it takes time. Hang in there. I'm pulling for you.

[Name] died [number] of months ago this week. Yet it's still hard to believe this powerful presence, this big smile and hearty laugh, this enveloping hug and font of wisdom, is gone from this earth. People tell us [his/her] spirit remains, but it isn't embodied in a tangible way anymore, and that's what we miss. I'm thinking of you today and remembering [him/her] with fondness and joy.

As the reality of your [relative's] absence sinks in, as you reach for the phone to call [him/her] before you realize [he/she] isn't there to answer, there will be times of intense sadness and grief. Over time, the bad times will become less frequent and the intensity will decrease. In the meantime, take each day as it comes, with

whatever relief, sadness, joy, or memories it may hold. I'm thinking of you.

The things that at first bring tears later bring smiles. I hope this [number]-month anniversary is bringing you some smiles along with the tears.

It's been over six months since [name] died. Most people probably expect you to be long over your grief. Yet you and I know better. We know that the reality is hitting home and, although the searing heat of pain may be diminishing, the sadness can ambush you at any time. Know that I am not one of those who expect you to be strong. I don't expect you to be "over it." I only hope that as each week passes you're able to feel whatever emotions arise and lean on those of us who care.

The one-year anniversary of [name's] death no doubt looms large in your thoughts. I imagine the past year has brought many tears interspersed with the everyday joys of life. It cannot be easy to turn the calendar and know that [name] is no longer only a phone call, e-mail, or visit away. Many grieving people report that the second year can be just as difficult, as the reality fully hits. I wish I could erase your grief and loneliness, but I cannot. What I can do is remind and reassure you of my constant friendship and willingness to listen. I will call you on Tuesday to see whether we can set up a time to have coffee together.

As you pass through the first anniversary of [name's] death, it must still seem impossible to imagine a future that doesn't include your beloved child. The circle of friends is moving on, growing up, and doing things your child won't do, and it hurts every time. At the same time, [name's] memory lives on in the hearts and minds of those who had the privilege of knowing [him/her], and they will be forever changed by that relationship. Those who loved [him/her] will never forget your child. As you move through the second year, I hope the pain eases and is balanced by a heart full of memories.

On this, the [number] anniversary of [name]'s death, I offer a single rose in [his/her] memory.

Time passes and seasons change. Love remains forever. I'm thinking of you on this [number] anniversary.

The people you love forever change you, and you are a different person because [name] was in your life. That is a memory worth embracing.

One life can make such a difference. [Name]'s certainly did. I remember with you.

You are in my thoughts [and prayers], especially now as you struggle through these first months without [name] by your side.

Some people think you heal from grief by forgetting, by "putting this behind you now and getting on with life." They're wrong. You never forget. You take the love and the lessons with you as you move into a future that is enriched by [name]'s memory. So today, on this [number] anniversary, I toast [name] and all that [he/she] brought to life. May we all live well enough to honor [his/her] memory.

I was always impressed with [name] and the way [he/she] lived life. I miss that example. Yet in the time since [he/she] died, I have been equally impressed with you. This is an incredibly painful and lonely experience, but you keep putting one foot in front of the other, determined that you will heal and honor [name]'s memory. I want to thank you for your fortitude and courage. I hope that when I inevitably face this situation myself, I'll cope as courageously as you have.

As I look back on the months since [name]'s death, I find myself hoping that I might be as fine and caring a person as [he/she] was. What

an inspiration! I remember [him/her] today with a smile.

A. A. Milne wrote, "There is something you must always remember: You are braver than you believe, stronger than you seem, and smarter than you think." In these months since [name]'s death, you have proven Milne's assertions. I feel privileged to walk with you as you heal from your grief and move forward into the future.

There's an old saying: "Friends are those who know the song in my heart and sing it to me when I forget." In the midst of grief, it's hard to remember or sing your song. In these months since [name] died, I hope I've helped you not only remember your song but also to write new verses. I believe [name] would be proud of all you've done and of all you'll still accomplish.

I know you're getting anxious to [sell the house/move to the retirement community/other major decision involving a change in location or lifestyle]. Yet you've lost so much already. Perhaps the last thing you need is more loss on top of it. If you're willing to wait, I'll try to help you be patient, so you can make decisions when they're necessary and move wisely into the future. No matter what you decide, though, I'm on your side now and always.

Holidays or Marker Days

When someone you love has died, the holidays are a time of intensely mixed emotions. There are moments when you enjoy yourself, smile, or even laugh. Yet <name>'s absence is always with you, and those lighter moments will be mixed with times of deep sadness. In the midst of the craziness, it's especially important to take care of yourself and renew your spirit. I hope the enclosed gift certificate for a massage helps you do just that. Use it when you feel stressed and isolated or when you simply want to be pampered. My thoughts are with you throughout this time.

The upcoming holiday season is likely to be especially difficult as you go through familiar rituals without [name's] presence. I've also learned that it's common for everybody around you—possibly even your family members—to avoid mentioning [his/her] name. Or perhaps others will try to cheer you by saying things like "Be happy . . . it's what [he/she] would want for you." No doubt, [name] deeply wants your happiness, but I hope you can allow yourself the mixture of emotions that come unbidden this time of year—from gladness for the family you have to profound sadness that there is someone missing from the festivities. Allow each emotion its due, and you'll make it through. I'll be thinking of you, and I'll be in touch.

The holidays are a tough time when the one you love can't be here to share them. I hope the enclosed gift card for a massage provides a moment of respite from the craziness and helps renew your spirit. I'm thinking of you.

For many grieving people, the anticipation leading up to a special day is worse than the actual day. As you approach [event or holiday], you may find yourself dreading the occasion and looking for a way out. The best advice I've heard is to plan how you want to mark the day. Some people want to be alone; others want to be with family or friends. Some want to be busy all day; others want quiet time to reflect, shed tears, and remember. Follow your own heart. Regardless of how you choose to spend the day, know that I hold you in my thoughts and care. I will be here as you continue to pass these milestone days and work toward a new future.

Today, on your birthday, you can't help but think about [name] and what it might be like if [he/she] were here. I remember two years ago when [name] was excited about the gift [he/she] had purchased for you. I'll never forget

that twinkle in [his\her] eye. In spite of [his/her] physical absence, may you see just a bit of that twinkle today as you remember the gift that [he/she] was to your life.

It's your birthday (or [name]'s birthday). While many people who care may surround you, it will be painful not to have that one special person there. Even though it hurts, I hope you can open your heart enough to take in the love that others have for you, so you can let their care carry you through the day.

This is your first [birthday/Valentine's Day/Memorial Day/ etc.] without [name]. It is sure to bring a mix of emotions as you remember and miss [him/her]. I'm thinking of you.

The upcoming [event] is sure to be difficult for you. You may be wondering how you will get through it. You may have to dig deep and tap into inner resources. Then remember the day is only twenty-four hours long. If you keep breathing and putting one foot in front of the other, it will pass and soon be behind you. Each time you make it through a tough situation, you're one step further along the path. As you heal, I'll do whatever I can to help you keep moving forward to find life again.

As we go through the holiday season, we'll all miss [name]. Yet no one will miss [him/her] more than you will. As you go through the ups and downs of these days, know that I'm in your corner. I'll do what I can to help you get through it and come out on the other side.

I won't wish you a happy holiday. I will wish you an honest holiday, where you're free to feel whatever you are feeling at the time without anyone else telling you otherwise. Do what seems right for you. Accept invitations, but feel free to change your mind or to leave early if you want. Be with others when it's comforting, but take time alone whenever you need it. No matter all the well-meaning advice, the path you take should be yours. I'll be in touch soon to check in and see how you're doing.

There are so many special days—anniversaries, birthdays, Valentine's Day, family gatherings. Do you sometimes feel that every time you turn around you have to steel yourself for something else? Yet each time, you make it through. You're surviving, and you will heal. Hang in there, and keep moving. I'm here for you.

These can be difficult days, and you must miss [him/her] a lot. I'm thinking of you, remembering with you, and pulling for you. Together, we'll keep moving forward day by day.

Do you remember a year ago when the pain was still so fresh? You've come so far since then! You've started forming new goals, and you've made important decisions to help you achieve them. I know it hasn't been easy, and at times, you've wanted to give up. I am inspired by your strength and resilience, and I'll do whatever I can to help you keep healing.

Today I wish you sunrise in the darkness, warmth in your heart, and peace in your soul. Remembering [name] and thinking of you.

Today, I hope that you're able to remember not just [name]'s death but also [his/her] life. Perhaps you can celebrate just a bit by treating yourself with this [chocolate/scones/other gift]. I'm thinking of you.

I remember [name] loved [flowers/tea/etc.]. On this day of memories and smiles mixed with loss and tears, I offer [flowers/tea/etc.] to you as a gift in [his/her] honor. May we both continue to live well enriched by [his/her] memory.

Death of a Sibling

The death of an older brother is the loss of a childhood "co-conspirator in adventure." While the schemes and shenanigans of childhood give way to the richer intimacy of adulthood, the simple bonds of childhood never go away. I hope that as you grieve [name's] death, you'll also remember the joy he brought to your life these many years. May you "conspire" to more adventures in memory of your brother.

When a younger sibling dies before you do, all seems wrong with the world. It's especially painful when it happens so abruptly. Thoughts of "Why not me?" are common. After all, you proudly protected this person through thick and thin (even though there probably were some altercations from time to time). Though no one can replace [name], know that my thoughts are with you as you fondly recall your years together and grieve through the heartache that this separation brings.

When you lose an older [brother/sister], no matter what age, it's normal to feel especially vulnerable because a "protector" is gone. Though we may never mention the "protector" mantle past childhood, the security provided by an older sibling is always there. As you adjust to life without [his/her] physical presence, may you retain the bond of love you developed through the many years when your big [brother/sister] was always looking out for you.

May the memory of [name's] devotion to you as a big [brother/sister] sustain you even while you mourn [his/her] death and honor [him/her] with your own well-lived life.

It's been said that sisters are angels in disguise. While your sister may now be among the angels, the here and now is still a time of deep sadness because she has died. I hope you can surround yourself with friends and family who will help you remember the gift of [name's] life even while you mourn her death. I join my care to theirs so perhaps you may find some comfort in knowing you're not alone.

From what you told me, everyone who knew your [brother/sister] respected and loved [him/her]. Although [name] is no longer physically present with you and this reality brings untold sadness, [his/her] spirit lives on through the quiet and unassuming generosity [he/she] extended to so many. I honor that spirit this week by donating my time to [organization] in [his/her] memory, that [his/her] legacy of caring may continue.

Except for a parent, a [brother/sister] is likely one of the longest relationships we'll ever have. When the relationship ends through death, an essential link to life and love ends too. Nobody will ever replace [name], but the bond you shared lives on in who you are because of [his/her] presence in your life. May that bond sustain you as you grieve. Know that I'm here for you.

I never had the joy of having a [sister/brother], and I can't fully understand what you must be going through right now. I know from what you've told me that [name] will be especially remembered for [his/her] _____. May the happy memories you and [he/she] made together bring solace to help balance the sadness.

Death of a Child

Nothing, nothing is as hard as the death of one's own flesh and blood. It simply doesn't seem possible. If I thought words could provide the comfort you needed, surely I would write every day. Yet words fall short. Although I cannot say or do anything that will take away your pain, I want you to know I am thinking of you during this time of profound grief. I'll do whatever I can to walk through it with you and help you.

[Name] touched so many lives, in spite of the shortness of years, and [name's] memory lives on in the hearts and minds of those who had the privilege of knowing [him/her].

It must seem impossible to imagine a future that doesn't include your beloved child. [His/Her] circle of friends will move on, grow up, and do things your child won't, and it's bound to hurt every time. As you venture into your new reality, know that I'm here for you for the long term. I'll do what I can to help you remember, listen, and work with you to build a meaningful future. I begin by making a donation to [organization] as a living memorial to your child, so that others will continue to be touched by [his/her] legacy.

I've heard there is no grief as deep as after the death of a child. I cannot begin to imagine what you're experiencing right now. I only know I'm here to help you through it, to guide you to wise decisions even when you can barely think, and to do whatever I can to make this difficult situation easier.

A child embodies our hopes and dreams and literally carries a bit of us into the future. When a child dies, those hopes and dreams die too. This makes your grief doubly hard, as you let go not only of [his/her] physical presence but of the vision you had for [his/her] life. I stand by you to help honor the memories of the past while building new hopes and dreams for a future that would make [name] proud.

As you cope with [name]'s death, your pain will sometimes crash into you like tsunami waves, and you may feel you might drown in it. Other times, it will wash onto shore with the tide, pulling the sand out from under your feet. While I can't take away your grief, I hope our work together helps you feel more anchored. As the storm passes, the future still awaits you. I'll do whatever I can to help you honor your child's memory by building a good one.

Death of a Parent

The death of a [mother/ father] is sometimes compared to the cutting of a kite string, setting you adrift. May [his/her] memory sustain you and [his/her] example inspire you as you continue the flight through this world on which [he/she] first launched you. When you feel an old familiar tug of your "kite," you'll know you're never fully cut off from your [mother/ father]'s love. That will endure forever.

A mother gives us breath itself, and when she dies, another arc in the circle of life is written upon our hearts and souls. As you grieve the death of your mother with your tears, may you also remember with your laughter and smiles the thousands of beautiful imprints she made on your life. My thoughts are with you.

Parents are our history, our anchor in time. Even if the relationship was problematic, when a [mother/ father] dies, our entire perspective changes. Although nothing can anchor you like your parents, I hope our friendship can help keep you grounded in love and care as you get accustomed to your new place in the world.

No matter what your age, when both of your parents have died, you are alone in a way you've never been before. You may even feel orphaned. As you take on the mantle of being the eldest generation in your family, I'll be here to stand with you, listen to you, and help you walk into a future that would make your parents proud.

Not everyone has a good relationship with [his/her] parents. Yet a parent's death has a deep impact on everyone. Now you face mixed emotions of sadness and relief, acknowledging the many years of hurt while also knowing it is impossible now to have the relationship with your [mother/father] you always hoped you could build. My friend, be assured that I'm here to listen if you want, to offer my help, and to support you as you try to build loving relationships and a worthy legacy to pass on to your own kids.

Terminal Illness

I can't imagine what the diagnosis of your [relative]'s disease is like for you. I can only imagine that perhaps you are grateful for the years you've had with [him/her] fully present, yet simultaneously deeply sad and fearful for [his/her] diminishing state. It must be incredibly difficult. I offer you a listening ear, plus all the knowledge I can gather to help you and your family maintain grace and dignity as you deal with this situation.

A serious diagnosis can imitate a dripping faucet. It's often simply there in the background, part of the fabric of your life that you try to live with or ignore. Other times, the ever-present dripping seems so loud and persistent that you think it'll drive you crazy. I wish there were a way to fix the faucet, but that's beyond my pay scale. Still, I'm by your side to do whatever I reasonably can to help, whether it's to curse the situation, drown out the dripping for a little while, or just sit with it. I'll call you early next week.

My sincerest hope for you is that [name]'s treatment will result in a long period of remission. You still have dreams, hopes, energy, and goals that long to be fulfilled. I'll do what I can to help you prepare for any outcome, though, so you can concentrate on enjoying life together for as long as you have it.

I was shocked to hear your diagnosis. I guess nothing ever prepares a person to hear news like this. If I feel like this, I can't imagine what it's like for you. As you look ahead into the blinding headlights, know that I'm here to help ensure you have the resources you need to handle it.

I was saddened to hear that the prognosis now is bleak. It has to be painful and discouraging to know that, despite your incredible efforts to beat this, it may be a battle you can't win. As you consider your options for the immediate future, remember that choosing to forgo further treatments isn't a sign that you're "giving up"; it's a courageous admission of reality and a decision that can allow you to live as fully as possible until you take your last breath. Remember too that even if there's nothing more that doctors can do to cure the illness, there is always something we can do for you. Caring people are here in various roles to help you live your remaining time and to help ensure you pass on a legacy of love. Know that I care, and I'm here to help you do both.

Death by Suicide

Every death brings a mixture of emotions, but death by suicide is particularly complex. The stigma is real, and the grief is profound. Emotions come swirling into your life with the power and intensity of a tornado, threatening to sweep you away. You may wonder whether you'll survive it. It can be immensely helpful to talk with others who understand as no one else can and to know you're not alone. I've enclosed information on an excellent support group and a competent counselor. Please don't face this alone. I'll continue to be in touch as a listening ear and a caring friend.

Suicide. It's hard even to say the word and almost impossible to attach it to someone you love. Often the experience is made worse because there are so many people who can't truly hear you, who make you feel ashamed or guilty, or who judge [name] for what [he/she] did. They may mean well, but they simply don't know any better. Rely instead on those who are willing to listen, to hold your pain, to shoulder your tears, and to embrace you where you are. I'd like to be one of those people for you. I'll check in with you on [date] to see if you'd welcome a visit or a conversation.

Although psychologists learn more about suicide all the time, you'll never be able to make sense of this. Even if you could, it wouldn't change what happened. It will be the biggest challenge of your life to work through [name]'s death and heal. Because I value you as a person and as a friend, I'll stand by you through it all. I'll always listen to the truth, even when it's hard, and do what I can to help. I'll call you soon.

Suicide is such a baffling thing. What would cause such a bright, promising young person to take [his/her] own life? Could we have prevented it? Didn't [he/she] realize what it would do to the family? There are too many questions and too few answers. As you work through the complex web of emotions and grief, I can serve as a referral source and as a safe and confidential ear. Know that I care deeply, and I will be in touch.

Nothing in your life can ever prepare you for a suicide. I imagine it still doesn't seem real, as if it's some kind of nightmare and you'll soon wake up. It certainly isn't the vision you had for [name] or for yourself. As you cope and find your way through this horrendously difficult time, you are never far from my thoughts [and always in my prayers].

Helen Keller said, "All that we love deeply becomes a part of us." Despite [name]'s death by suicide, you clearly loved [him/her] deeply. The pain and grief you feel will take a long time and hard work to heal, and some of the love may seem overtaken by anger or guilt. In the end, though, the love is what will remain. [Name] will always have a place in your heart and in mine.

Longer Texts: Letters for Various Intervals

You may want to send a letter instead of a card, especially for clients you know well. The approximate timing is a guideline, although you can send any of these letters in the first two years following a death.

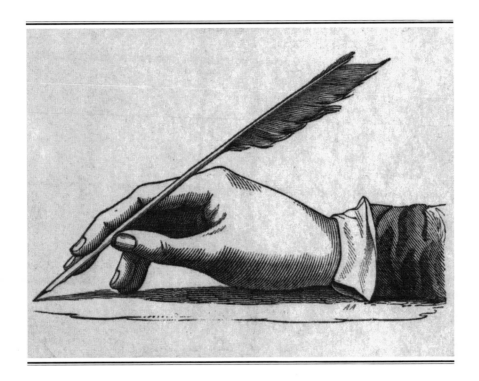

"Although our world is full of suffering, it is also full of the overcoming of it."

– Helen Keller

Recovery from grief is not a station you arrive at, but a manner of traveling.

–Dr. Ivan G. Mattern

Dear _____,

The funeral is over, and people have gone home. The harsh reality is sinking in. (Name) has died, and life will never be the same.

For many grieving people, this is a hard time. You may find yourself feeling angry, empty, and lonely. Friends may not understand or may no longer want to hear your pain. You may be unsure of yourself or unable to concentrate or find stability. In fact, you may wonder whether you're going crazy.

First, we assure you that you are not going crazy. What you're experiencing is normal for a grieving person.

Grief is a process of creating a memory out of what can no longer be and moving into a future that is very different from the one you planned. It isn't easy, and it takes a long time. It's tempting to make it "go away" by keeping yourself too busy to think or feel. Yet grief is persistent, and it will force itself back into your life. It's best to deal with it as it comes to you, even though it may be raw and painful, so you continue to move forward.

Here are some things you can do:

1. Ignore people who say you "should" feel this or you "should" put it behind you and get on with your life. Feel whatever you feel now; grieve on your own timetable.

2. Go to the cemetery if it's comforting; don't go if it isn't. Cry when you need to; laugh when you want. Express your emotions so they don't become trapped inside.

3. Forgive yourself for anything you regret, whether it was not saying goodbye, losing your temper, or wishing you'd done things differently. You did the best you could with what you had at the time; that's all anyone can expect. It's OK to forgive and let go.

4. Take care of yourself physically. Commit to getting enough sleep, eating healthy foods (with an occasional indulgence thrown in!), and exercising reasonably. Soak in a hot tub. Get a massage. Breathe deeply.

5. Find at least one person in whom you can honestly confide, and talk with him or her regularly.

6. Plan at least one enjoyable activity a week, and follow through even when you don't feel like it.

7. Make a list of the things you're thankful for and keep it handy. When you're having a bad day, it helps to remember that all of life isn't bad.

8. Reach out to someone else who's hurting or in need.

9. Read the wisdom of others. Use the library, the Internet, and bookstores to search out good resources.
10. Rely on your sense of spirituality in whatever way is meaningful to you, allowing your inner self to find consolation.

We'll stay in regular contact with you this year because we know how hard grief can be. We also know that eventually the sun will shine in your heart and you will heal. We'll do whatever we can to help that happen while we guard your financial stability.

We are here for you.

Sincerely,

There is a sacredness in tears. They are not the mark of weakness but of power. They speak more eloquently than ten thousand tongues. They are messengers of overwhelming grief, of deep contrition, and of unspeakable love.

–*Washington Irving*

Dear _____,

By now, you've probably experienced the "roller coaster effect" of grief. Just when you feel you're healing—you have more energy, you feel lighter than before, and you're relieved to be finally through the worst—suddenly you spiral down again.

These unwelcome events can be triggered by seeing someone who looks like <name> or hearing a certain song, or there may be no discernible trigger at all. You just know you were feeling better, and now you're feeling lousy again. Many people begin to wonder whether they're healing at all, whether they will ever recover, or whether they're doomed to grinding pain for the rest of their lives.

I hope it helps you to know that you're healing in a normal and expected way. Healing is not a linear process, where you feel incrementally better until you completely heal. It's more like a roller coaster, going up and down repeatedly. Another analogy sometimes used is an onion—you deal with continual layers of grief, each one getting closer to the center of your pain and plunging you temporarily back into the abyss.

Studies have shown that it's extremely common to experience a serious "down time" starting anywhere from four to nine months after someone you love dies. The numbness or shock has worn off, and reality stares you squarely in the face. It is a stressful and often emotional period.

When you experience this, don't give up. Rather than regressing, you're healing a little bit deeper. Each time you go through a difficult period, face a holiday, or handle a painful situation, you get stronger. Each time you spiral down, the pain you endure is stretching you and helping you heal. You are not going back to ground zero. It's more like two steps forward and one back, then three steps forward and one or two back. You are progressing, actually getting somewhere; the process of grief just doesn't happen in a straight line.

Keep your hope alive, even when it's just barely flickering. Over time, the world will brighten for you again, you'll notice yourself smiling more and crying less, and the intensity of your grief will decrease. Life is still a marvelous gift, and you have a lot of living to do. We'll do whatever we can to support you in your grief journey.

We're here for you.

Sincerely,

I walked a mile with pleasure; she chattered all the way,

But left me none the wiser for all she had to say.

I walked a mile with sorrow; And ne'er a word said she;

But, oh, the things I learned from her when sorrow walked with me!

–Robert Browning Hamilton

Dear _____,

In some ways, it seems like just yesterday that <name> died. In other ways, it seems like an eternity.

Over time, many grieving people find themselves thinking about things that were left unresolved. One widow never got to say goodbye to her husband before he did. One man's last words to his son were angry. A woman knew she and her sister had hurt each other, but they didn't have time to work it out before her sister died in an accident.

One technique many grievers find helpful is writing a letter to their deceased loved one. You can say everything you need to say, tell of your pain now, acknowledge any pain you caused, forgive and ask for forgiveness. Hold nothing back. Then do what makes sense with the letter. You can bury it at the gravesite, burn it in a fireplace, tear it into little shreds, store it in a memory box, or whatever else feels right to you.

Many grieving people also find it helpful to keep a journal. You don't have to be an experienced writer. Just buy a notebook and make an entry every day. Spell out your anger, fear, struggles, insights, and joys, knowing that no one else ever has to read it. Your notebook is constantly available as a safe, accessible outlet for your experience. In fact, some mourners find it helpful to write just before bed, to prevent waking up in the middle of the night full of unexpressed thoughts or feelings. As an added bonus, when you get discouraged and think you haven't made any progress, you can look back and see how far you've come.

Another tip that helps many people is to make at least one new beginning. Learn a new hobby, take a class that interests you, plan a trip to a new location, or grow plants you've never grown before. Choose an activity you can relish and anticipate, and do it regularly.

You may or may not find these techniques useful. We offer them as simple suggestions because they've helped others who have lost loved ones. Whether you use these ideas or others, we hope you find that life is still worth living, that there is much to explore and learn, and that in spite of the trials and pain, this world is still a fascinating and wonderful place. Your life will never be the same, but it can be good again.

We're here for you.

Sincerely,

These, then, are my last words to you: Be not afraid of life.
Believe that life is worth living, and your belief will help create the fact.

–William James

Dear _____,

Though it hardly seems possible, soon it will be a year since <name> died. This first anniversary is usually a deeply sensitive time. Be aware of "anniversary anxiety," where dreadful anticipation causes the days before the anniversary to be more stressful than the day itself. Be assured that although the day marks a painful milestone, it will pass, and you will make it through.

It can be helpful to plan what you want to do that day. Here are a few ideas that have worked for others. Gather with significant people at your home to remember, cry, hug, and eat together. Go out for part or all of the day. If it's a workday, you may want to maintain that part of your normal routine, or perhaps you wish to just be alone. It may be comforting to visit the cemetery or attend services at your church. There is no "right" way to observe the anniversary. Decide what you need and want to do, and then let others know your wishes so they don't surprise you with something you don't want.

The anniversary is also a good time to take stock of the last twelve months. You made it through all the "firsts"— the first holiday season, the first birthday, etc.—and you survived. You grew and changed as a person, becoming more appreciative, aware, tolerant, and compassionate. In spite of the pain you still feel, you healed tremendously and are less likely to take life or relationships for granted.

Your grief isn't resolved yet. The second year will carry its own type of pain as the reality fully sets in. You'll encounter people who say "Surely you're healed by now" or "It's been a whole year—why do you still cry?" They'll tell you to put it behind you and get on with life. They simply don't understand that, in many ways, grief is a lifelong process. It won't continue to be as fresh or raw, and your sad times will become less frequent and less intense until they're only sporadic. Yet you'll never forget someone you loved this much. You'll never stop missing them or wondering what life would be like if they were still alive. For the rest of your life, even if you haven't cried in years, there will be times when you are ambushed and the will tears flow again.

Try to trust yourself and your gradual healing process more than you listen to well-meaning but uninformed people. Remember in ways that make sense to you, even if others don't understand. We will support you as your journey toward peace and healing continues through the coming year.

We are here for you.

Sincerely,

*Lost irreversibly in objective time, the person is present in a new form within one's
mind and heart, tenderly present in inner time without the pain and bitterness of death.
And once the loved one has been accepted in this way,
he or she can never again be forcefully removed.*

– R.C. Cantor

Dear _____,

This isn't a particular anniversary or marker day, but we wanted to let you know that even though it has been more than a year since <name> died, we still remember.

Sometimes people think that to remember a person you have to visualize every detail of their physical appearance. Those people panic, as details inevitably get fuzzy.

Instead, realize that the most important memory you have of <name> lies within. You are a different person because <he/she> loved you, and no one can ever take that away. You will forever carry with you all that <name> meant to you, all that <he/she> taught you, and all that you've become as a result. These are the memories worth hanging onto, even as you create new tomorrows.

You can honor <name> by choosing to live as fully and vibrantly as you can, enriched by <his/her> memory.

We will help you do that as we work together to protect your financial stability and achieve your goals. Together we'll remember but continue to move forward.

We are here for you.

Sincerely,

CORGENIUS

ADDING HEART TO THE BRAINS OF BUSINESS

Recently, a man wrote of the crisis he went through when he turned fifty. He realized his life might be half over or more, yet there was so much he still wanted to do and experience. He started to feel the preciousness of time and the compulsion to make the most of whatever he had left. It caused him to re-evaluate how he spent his time, what he spent his money on, and which things and people were truly important in his life. He read books, pondered, and finally made some decisions that, in big and small ways, changed the way he lived.

When his wife was diagnosed and then died of cancer eight years later, he was awash in grief. He couldn't imagine life without her: his emotions seemed out of control, and he wanted her back. Gradually, as he came to accept the fact that he couldn't have her back and that her death was now a permanent fixture of his life, he also realized that he was still alive.

He realized anew that life is transient and unpredictable: he could have many years left, or he could get a bad diagnosis next week. Even more powerfully than his fiftieth birthday had, his wife's death woke him up to the preciousness of time and the unknown amount he h as left.

Prompted by this knowledge, he is once again in the process of re-evaluating his life, although this time without her by his side. He is thinking hard about what gives him enjoyment, what gifts he can share with others, how he can make a difference and live with meaning, who and what are truly important, where he spends money, and how he spends the minutes of his day.

Everything has changed for him, and he is doing his best to consciously, reflectively, and prayerfully change with it. He wants to carry his wife's love with him and find ways to give that love to others on her behalf. Knowing he may have much or only a little time left, he wants to honor his wife by living his own life as fully as possible.

This is easier said than done, and some days he just wants to hide in bed or die himself. Yet he remembers her, and it keeps him putting one foot in front of the other. It keeps him talking to supportive people so he can process his grief, and it keeps him searching for new goals in his life. He grieves with hope.

No matter who or what you have lost, you are still alive. There can be joy and happiness ahead if you choose it. The pain is real and intense, but healing is possible. Each morning, try to make one more small decision for life. Grieve, but with hope.

Articles for Clients

You may wish to send articles to some clients, especially if they are struggling with a particular aspect of their grief. These are possibilities to consider. Reading through them may also increase your personal understanding.

A Positive Decision on Love

We were in a seminar on grief. The bitter impact of loss was tangible. One man said that if his wife died, he could see no reason to ever remarry. "I would make a positive decision not to love again—to close off the possibility of remarriage so as to avoid that pain a second time."

"A positive decision not to love again." The words stuck in my throat as I tried to make them palatable enough to swallow. It didn't work. There are valid reasons for turning away from the possibility of a love relationship. In some religious traditions, vowed celibates will turn away from physical love to more fully dedicate their lives to God. Singles will turn away from promiscuity to maintain their integrity. Married couples will turn away from adultery to preserve their marriage. Yet is it possible for a person to reject the possibility of loving deeply again to avoid the pain?

My mind drifted back to my own experience. John and I had been married for five years. After suffering the pain of two miscarriages, we finally welcomed a beautiful baby boy into our family. We held each other at night and felt like the luckiest people on earth. One icy February night, when our son was seven months old, that luck evaporated. John was on his way home from a meeting when another car slammed broadside into his; he was killed instantly. In that split second, my life changed forever.

From the time John died, I told everyone, including myself, that I hoped to marry again. I reasoned that my experience of marriage had been a positive one, and I wanted that level of intimate relationship again. I also wanted our son, Carl, to have brothers and sisters. In retrospect, though, I realize the main reason I wanted to marry again was that marriage was the style of life I knew, and it was comfortable.

I had never lived on my own. I grew up in a large family, sharing my bedroom with three sisters. I went to college and had two room-mates. At nineteen, I married John. When he died, I didn't know what it was like to have a room to myself, much less a child, much less a life. I was lost, looking for someone to come in and take over for me—to lead, protect, and guide me. My desire to marry again was borne of fear—the fear of being alone, the fear of being a single parent, and the fear of failure when there was no one to blame but me.

At first, I didn't consciously recognize those fears. Actually, in the initial months, I had no time to think of relationships anyway. The funeral, estate decisions, insurance, and probate took much of my energy. I spent the rest trying to hold myself together. I lived with intense pain. I longed to laugh, to be whole, and to feel as if I had some control over my life. I cried out to God to give me strength or give me death because I couldn't go on as I was. I also had Carl to consider. He didn't have a dad anymore, so he'd better have a mom. For both of our sakes I had to heal, and I wanted to heal more than I had ever wanted anything in my life.

I was determined to face my grief head on. I prayed hard, sometimes railing against God and the unfairness of John's death, and other times resting my exhausted heart in the palm of God's hand. I read everything I could find about grief. I talked with friends, family, and anyone who would listen. I forced myself to go places where John and I used to go, to do things we used to do, to face every situation that would remind me again that he was dead and that I was alone. Sometimes I thought I would break, but each

time I survived intact it was another victory. I gradually felt a sense of accomplishment and self-worth.

I did not "leave John behind" and get on with my life; I took my treasured memories with me, always aware that I would forever be a different person because John loved me. Slowly, I began letting go of the future John and I had so carefully planned, grieving for the dreams that would never be realized. At the same time, I began to build a new future for myself. I became involved in things I hadn't done before: coordinating the parish youth group, joining a community chorus, and taking computer classes. Each step increased my confidence and helped me discover strengths and talents I didn't know I had.

I dated quite a few people in the years after John died, two of whom wanted to marry me. Although I cared about them a great deal, and I reveled in their hugs, kisses, and affection, I did not love them as life mates. Sadly, because I was so hungry for the attention and security they offered, I dated them longer than I should have, fooling both of us into believing a future together was possible. Yet I knew in my heart that something wasn't right, and eventually I broke off each relationship.

I still thought about marrying again, but I was discovering the advantages and freedoms of being single. Solitude was teaching me a great deal about myself and what I desired. I was growing in compassion, strength, patience, and tolerance. I took time for spirituality and felt my faith deepen. I was involved in things that were fulfilling to me. I became increasingly content with my life as a single person and a single parent. I was healing, I was becoming happier and more whole, and it felt good.

There's a poem about a butterfly. It says that if you chase the butterfly, it will constantly elude you, but if you sit and mind your own business, it will land on your shoulder. My butterfly's name was Ken. Neither of us had a serious relationship in mind. Ken was in a college seminary. I was six years older, a widow with a young child and quite content to be single. Any thought of the two of us together was preposterous.

It was that safety—the "knowing" that nothing could happen between us—that resulted in our growing close. There was no risk or pressure, just a couple of good friends sharing their thoughts and feelings in complete freedom. After about a year, we came to realize that we were deeply in love with each other. Once we overtly acknowledged our feelings, we decided to marry.

By then, almost four years had passed since John had died. I had worked through much grief and felt that I had some sense of completion about it. So I was shocked to discover the panic that welled up as I comprehended what marrying Ken meant. I knew in the depths of my being and with a certainty borne of experience that Ken was going to die. The only questions were which of us would die first and when. I was terrified. Could I risk it again? Could I freely leave myself open to that kind of hell? Could I put Carl in the potential position of having two dads die?

I found myself refusing to envision us together at age fifty. I would not envision us with grand-children. I convinced myself that there was a part of my heart that would always be John's, a part that Ken could not have. In the crucible of fear, I knew that if I didn't allow myself to dream and plan a future, I would not be so devastated if it never came to be. If I didn't give my whole heart and commit myself 100 percent, then even if Ken died, a part of me would remain intact and unscathed. I shook with terror, and hot tears coursed down my face. Oh, God, just tell me he's not going to die! Just tell me that this time it will last forever!

Ken saw and gently confronted me with the things I did not want to face. In light of my fears, we both knew that I had to make a choice. I could be safe and self-reliant, giving no more than I was willing to lose to death. If that were my choice, I would indeed spare myself the pain of surviving another husband's death, but I would lose my life with Ken. The alternative was to open my heart wide, loving deeply and fiercely with no reservations. I would open myself to tremendous pain but also to tremendous joy. The decision was mine.

I was trembling. I could barely breathe. Yet I knew who I wanted to be and how I wanted to live. I chose Ken. We were married a few months later.

Today, two decades later, I still know the swiftness with which death can strike. In my heart, I know that Ken could die tonight and I could once again be plunged into the abyss of grief. If that occurred, would I still believe that marrying him was the right decision?

My soul cries, "Yes!" Whenever it comes, Ken's death will bring the absolute depths of sorrow into my life, but that is only because I have experienced the absolute heights of joy with him. I cannot have one without the other. I will be in agony, I will scream and cry, and I will be stretched as thin as blown glass, but I will have loved with my whole being. I will have lived—truly lived.

The key is the motivation behind the decision. My choice—single, vowed celibate, or married—must reflect my firm belief that to live that lifestyle would call forth the best in me. It must require me to love deeply and completely, to take risks, to grow, and to use the life I am given in the truest way possible. I cannot cut myself off from any particular kind of love, living "safely" for the rest of my life, without concurrently cutting myself off from the exuberant dance of joy that springs from the heart of deep love.

A positive decision not to love again? No, that is impossible. As all my excuses were, it is an excuse borne of fear. The fears may be as varied and complex as the people involved. Yet when presented with the opportunity to truly and deeply love, a decision to ignore, reject, or destroy that love is not a positive decision. It robs us of the vibrancy and challenge of life.

It is death victorious.

Anything and Everything, Except the Obvious

How often does it happen? You get together with family or friends, and you're having a good time. Yet after a while, you notice that people are talking about everything and everyone EXCEPT the person who died, even when it would be natural to include something about him or her in the conversation. They all tiptoe around it and avoid even mentioning the person's name. Why is everyone so afraid?

The truth is, they are well meaning but uninformed. They are afraid that if they say the name, they will make you sad or spoil your evening. They think it is their job to cheer you up or take your mind off the reality.

They don't realize it is not their job to "fix it." They can't take your grief away anyway: the loss is always in your mind, no matter how hard others try to move it away. Nor do they realize how much you long to hear the name, how badly you want to know that someone besides you remembers, or how hungry you are for the stories and memories they could share.

They can be much more comforting if they can acknowledge and accept your sadness, give you an understanding smile or a hug, or even cry with you. Shared grief diminishes, but grief that is repressed or denied festers inside until it finds a way to come out.

Besides, tears are healthy. Despite our fears to the contrary, no one in the history of the world has ever started crying and not been able to stop. Most people report feeling relieved, freed, or even cleansed after a good cry. In addition, tears contain physiological chemicals that relieve stress; we are supposed to cry when we are sad.

So what can you do when people are afraid to say the name? The easiest thing is to say the name yourself. Bring up a story or a memory that involves your spouse whenever it seems to fit. That gives others permission to say the name too.

You can even address the issue explicitly, saying, "You know, sometimes people are afraid to mention the name for fear of making me sad. Yet I love to hear it and to share in your stories and memories. Please don't be afraid."

If you do start to cry, say something like, "Don't worry. You did not make me cry. The tears are there anyway, and every once in a while they spill over. It's okay. Please don't let my tears make you stop talking about your memories. I love to know that someone else remembers too."

You will still find that some people are uncomfortable with your grief and sadness. In their presence, you may have to go along with the illusion that you are happy and that everything is fine. There will be others, though, with whom you can freely share whatever you are experiencing. Friends who can hear you, hug you, cry with you, and walk through grief with you are priceless treasures. With them, you can truly have a good time.

Chasing After Closure

I keep reading in the newspapers about survivors of tragedy or death seeking "closure." Yet no one really defines what closure means, whether it is possible, or how to get there.

For many in our society, closure means leaving grief behind, a milestone usually expected within a matter of weeks or months. Closure means being "normal": getting back to your old self and no longer crying or being affected by the death. It means "moving on with life" and leaving the past behind, even to the extent of forgetting it or ignoring it. For those of us who have experienced death, this kind of closure is not only impossible but also indeed undesirable.

Closure, if one even chooses to use the term, is more of a process than a defined moment. The initial part of closure is accepting the reality. At first, we keep hoping or wishing that it weren't true. We expect our loved one to walk through the door. We wait for someone to tell us it was all a huge mistake. We just can't accept that this person has died, that we will never physically be together again on earth, or that we will not hear the voice, feel the hug, or get the person's input on a tough decision. Usually, it takes weeks or even months for the reality to finally sink in. We come to know, in both our heads and in our hearts, that our loved one has died and is not coming back. We still don't like it, but we accept it as true.

As the reality sinks in, we can more actively heal. We begin making decisions and start to envision a life different from what we had planned before, a life in which we no longer expect our loved one to be there. We grow, struggle, cry, and change. We form fresh goals. We face our loneliness. We feel the pain and loss, but except for short periods, we are not crippled by it. We also make a shift in memory. Memories of our loved one, rather than being painful as they were at first, sometimes make us smile or even laugh.

This healing phase takes a long time, and it involves a lot of back-and-forthing. We alternate between tears and joy, fears and confidence, and despair and hope. We take two steps forward and one step back. We wonder whether we'll ever be truly happy again and often doubt that we will.

Eventually, we realize we are taking the past, with all its pain and pleasure, into a new tomorrow. We never forget, and in fact, we carry our beloved with us; he or she is forever a cherished part of who we are. We are changed by the experience of having loved this person, by the knowledge of life's transience, and by grief itself. We become different and hopefully better—more compassionate, more appreciative, more tolerant—people. We fully embrace life again, connecting, laughing, and loving with a full heart.

Still, there is no point of "final closure," no point at which you can say, "Ah, now I have finally completed my grief" or "Yes, now I have healed." Or "I will never miss him again, or wonder what life would be like if he were still alive." There is no point at which you will never cry again, although as time goes on, the tears are bittersweet and less common. Healing is a lifelong process, one in which you often don't even realize you are healing until you look back and see how far you've come.

Closure? I don't think so. Acceptance—yes. Peace—yes. Hope—definitely. Putting a period behind the final sentence and closing the book on it? No, life and love are much too complex for that. The story does not end; instead, it awaits the next chapter.

The Starting Point—Filling the Emptiness

Dave Barry wrote, "My psychologist tells me it is more satisfying to finish what I've started. He's right. Today I've finished two bags of M&M's and a chocolate cake, and I feel better already." If you're a person who regularly goes for a "chocolate fix," this quote could make you chuckle. However, it also points out our love/hate relationship with food, especially when we're grieving.

When you feel that familiar gnawing pain in your gut—that unsettled empty void—it's so easy to go for the comfort foods: ice cream, chocolate, biscuits and gravy, a juicy steak, or anything else that seems like it will "fill up" the emptiness or "stuff down" those pesky emotions that keep welling up. Perhaps instead you go for a glass of wine (or two or three), a few beers, or a stiff martini. Another common alternative is drowning out the pain with absorbing work, intense exercise, endless Internet searches and YouTube videos, or an overly busy schedule.

Unfortunately, none of these things works for long. You aren't really longing for chocolate, and you're not hungry for food. Alcohol only covers up the pain temporarily. After the work or the frenzied activity is done, the grief awaits you.

Pushing down the grief, denying it, or covering it up will not make it go away. In fact, suppressed grief simply festers inside and waits for an opportunity to show itself. It may come out in physical ways—headaches, neck aches, backaches, or stomachaches. It may come out in psychological ways like outbursts of anger, impatience with people who don't deserve it, depression, or suicidal thoughts. Perhaps saddest—because so much repressed grief and hurt lurks inside—is a life that is never truly joyful again or a person who has an inability to love deeply again.

It is certainly a lot more difficult to confront the loss than to indulge in a hot fudge sundae. Yet, to heal, you need to avoid that temptation to cover it up, push it down, deny its existence, or pretend it is something that it's not. Instead, we hope you can find the courage to express the sadness: remember your beloved, tell someone about the void, cry whenever you feel the need, write, pound nails, or find some other way to express and process what you're experiencing.

When you face the pain honestly and work through it with the help of supportive people, you will eventually heal. You may also find that as you quit substituting false fixes, a hot fudge sundae can be even more enjoyable because it's a treat and not a leaky bandage.

Can you trust the process more than you trust your favorite comfort foods? Can you avoid the phony, temporary, illusive solutions in favor of those that will bring lasting healing and happiness? And along the way, don't forget that you can still have a few M&M's.

Grieve with Hope

Recently, a man wrote of the crisis he went through when he turned fifty. He realized his life might be half over (or more), yet there was so much he still wanted to do and experience. He started to feel the preciousness of time and the compulsion to make the most of whatever he had left. It caused him to re-evaluate how he spent his time, what he spent his money on, and which things and people were truly important in his life. He read books, pondered, and finally made some decisions that, in big and small ways, changed the way he lived.

When his wife was diagnosed with cancer and died of it eight years later, he was awash in grief. He couldn't imagine life without her: his emotions seemed out of control, and he wanted her back. Gradually, as he came to accept the fact that he couldn't have her back and that her death was now a permanent fixture of his life, he also realized that he was still alive.

He realized anew that life is transient and unpredictable: he could have many years left, or he could get a bad diagnosis next week. Even more powerfully than his fiftieth birthday had, his wife's death woke him up to the preciousness of time and the unknown amount he has left.

Prompted by this knowledge, he is once again in the process of re-evaluating his life, although this time without her by his side. He is thinking hard about what gives him enjoyment, what gifts he can share with others, how he can make a difference and live with meaning, who and what are truly important, where he spends money, and how he spends the minutes of his day.

Everything has changed for him, and he is doing his best to consciously, reflectively, and prayerfully change with it. He wants to carry his wife's love with him and find ways to give that love to others on her behalf. Knowing he may have much or only a little time left, he wants to honor his wife by living his own life as fully as possible.

This is easier said than done, and some days he just wants to hide in bed or die himself. Yet he remembers her, and it keeps him putting one foot in front of the other. It keeps him talking to supportive people so he can process his grief, and it keeps him searching for new goals in his life. He grieves with hope.

No matter who or what you have lost, you are still alive. There can be joy and happiness ahead if you choose it. The pain is real and intense, but healing is possible. Each morning, try to make one more small decision for life. Grieve, but with hope.

How to Handle Your Fears After the Death of a Spouse

We have the opportunity to face what is there—ourselves . . . We will find that we're less than we wish, as imperfect as we feared. But having faced that . . . we free ourselves. New energies will be released within the creative part of us, the part that wants to grow, the part that is ready to reach beyond . . . We begin to feel less anguish and more comfort, less threat and more promise. The promise is that by living fully our aloneness, we can become more whole. We can become more who we were meant to be.

– James Miller, *A Pilgrimage Through Grief*

"For so long I experienced life as John and Amy, as Mr. and Mrs. Now I am just Amy. Amy alone. No John by my side. And I am terrified."

I wrote this journal entry about two weeks after another car slammed broadside into my husband's, killing him instantly. In that moment, death slammed broadside into my life, and I had to learn to let go of the one person I thought I could never live without. I felt many things: anxiety, sadness, gratitude, loneliness, anger, and more. As I looked ahead, though, there was one overriding emotion: fear. I didn't know where to turn or who to count on. I felt unable to make decisions, incapable of even the simplest tasks.

I have since learned that fear, like grief, need not dominate your life or last forever. When we express and honestly deal with fears, they eventually resolve, leaving hope for peace, healing, and even joy.

So let's look at some fears that come with the territory and share suggestions for coping. Although your grief is individual and unique, perhaps some of these tips will work for you.

Build a New Normal
Three months after John's death, I said to a friend, "I'm scared to look ahead. When those two cars hit, all our plans and dreams evaporated, and there is nothing left. My entire future got wiped out in an instant."

My friend wisely said, "No, Amy, your future was not wiped out. John's was, at least on this earth. You still have a future; it's just going to be very different than you thought." Her words pierced through the fog. She was right.

The next evening, I looked back at goals I'd written in my journal. Some were directly related to John, but others were not. I wanted to vacation at the ocean, audition for the community theater, and work with the church youth group. I dreamed of taking voice lessons and someday publishing a book. There were still goals I could reach and things I could do, if I so chose. I could never go "back to normal"—that "normal" would never exist again. Yet perhaps I could build a "new normal" that fit me. It wouldn't be the same without John, but for the first time, I dared to think that maybe it could still be good. There was some continuity. Not all was gone. I did indeed have a future.

Face the Emotions
C.S. Lewis wrote, "No one ever told me that grief felt so like fear." Because it is scary to confront grief, many widowed people avoid solitude like the plague. They obey the "standard wisdom" that says you should keep busy and not think about it. Granted, a certain amount of busyness is a good thing. It is healthy to grieve in spurts, allowing yourself time to relax, to breathe, and even to laugh. Yet we need balance because grief doesn't go away until you deal with your emotions.

Take time to name and express your feelings. I wrote in a journal every night. Sometimes I sat on the "pity pot" temporarily, feeling sorry for myself, whining, or throwing an old-fashioned temper tantrum on the floor. Perhaps you prefer to pound nails into wood. You can sketch, scribble, or use finger paints. Some people make something out of clay or Play-Doh and then decide whether to smash it or keep it. None of this has to be "good," and no one ever has to see it. It just has to get the emotions out.

Through it all, go ahead and cry. It is common to fear that once you start crying, you won't be able to stop. But that has never happened in the history of humankind. You'll be OK. In fact, you'll be more OK than before. There are physiological chemicals in tears that relieve stress.

Finally, when your emotions are spent for now, do something comforting. I loved to light candles and soak in a hot bath. Perhaps you'd like to eat fresh popcorn or listen to classical music. Some people take comfort in a cup of tea, a brisk walk or swim, or simply standing outside and breathing deeply of the fresh air. It feels good and helps restore some of the energy that grief siphons off.

Find New Friends
Many widowed people rightly fear that they no longer fit into their social circles. If you have known a couple for a long time, they may remain good friends, providing stability even as others fall away. For the most part, though, your life has changed, and your network of friends eventually reflects that fact. You need to build new connections, particularly among unmarried people.

The most comfortable relationships, especially initially, are with other widowed people. After all, they understand your experience. Check your place of worship, hospice, or hospital for support groups. It takes courage to attend, but it

is well worth it. The people there will nod their heads and affirm your feelings; they've been there too. It provides a nonthreatening way to create new support and friendship networks. Like you, most of them are looking for someone to have coffee with, a group to see a movie with, or a phone number they can call when it's a rough day.

Be Safe
Everyone who lives alone knows that houses creak and groan, especially in the middle of the night. Movies and TV shows play off the horror of confronting a lunatic with a weapon. Rather than being overcome by fear, take reasonable steps to increase your safety. If you don't have one, install a home alarm. Have outside lights on motion sensors. Always lock doors, regardless of whether you're home. Ensure that windows are secure and that sliding doors have security bars.

Some people turn on a TV to have a voice in the house, or they play music that provides noise and relaxes them at the same time. Keep pepper spray on your nightstand and have another on your keychain to carry with you.

You may want to take a self-defense class at a local community college or park district. Practicing the techniques is good exercise, and interacting with other people is good for your spirit. It will also help you regain a sense of strength and control.

Discover Yourself
So much of your identity and routine were intertwined with your spouse that it's hard to know who you are by yourself. You can feel vulnerable and exposed.

If you are open, though, you may begin to discover the freedom and adventure of being on your own. For instance, one woman's husband would only eat butter pecan ice cream, so that's all she ever bought. After he died, she wanted to find the ice cream she liked best. She discovered two favorites: mint chocolate chip and rocky road. She still occasionally has butter pecan in memory of her husband, but now she knows something about herself she didn't know before. It was one small step in discovering her new identity.

It is amazing to find out how many things you can do. I learned how to mow the lawn and do simple plumbing repairs. I got a device to help open tight jar lids. I painted the bedroom a different color. For areas where I didn't feel competent, I got help. For instance, I asked friends until I found a good handyman and a trustworthy financial advisor.

As I learned and grew, I became stronger and more confident in myself. Of course, I still missed John, wished he were there, and sometimes resented being alone. But I also came to know I could survive without him and perhaps one day even enjoy life again.

Imagine the Worst
It may seem counterintuitive, but sometimes the most helpful way to handle fears is to imagine the worst that could possibly happen and then decide whether you could survive it. What is the worst scenario, for instance, if you don't have enough money to keep your house?

Even though you don't want to, could you survive if you had to get an apartment or move in with a grown child? Chances are good that no matter the consequences of your fears, you would still be OK if the worst happened. That knowledge can take away some of fear's power. You can cope. You can go on. You can survive.

Heal
Healing takes longer than you imagine. Sometimes you take three steps forward and two steps back. For many people, the second year is as hard as the first, just in different ways. But gradually, the memories bring smiles instead of tears, and you take the past with you into a new tomorrow. You never forget; you carry your beloved with you forever as a cherished part of who you are, yet you grow and become a more compassionate, appreciative, and tolerant person. As you keep facing your fears, you will learn to embrace life again, connecting, laughing, and loving with a full heart.

Keeping Busy

I can't count the number of times I've asked people how they cope with grief and they say, "Well, I keep myself busy."

Keeping busy can be a good thing. We all need to have a purpose, a reason to get out of bed in the morning. We all have gifts and talents to share, and we are called to offer them to others. We all need enough money to live, and most of the time staying employed makes that possible.

However, you need to make sure that keeping busy doesn't become the excuse that keeps you from grieving. It is easy to fill every hour with activity to avoid facing the fact that you are alone. It is easy to wear yourself out so thoroughly that you are too exhausted to think about what has happened.

Our society feeds the tendencies to stay busy because we value productivity and deny pain. After a tragedy, you are expected to pick yourself up and move on. You are told not to be a burden and not to bring everybody else down. You are told that it's time you put this behind you and get on with life.

Give yourself permission to ignore society. Give yourself plenty of time and space to grieve. Cry until you think you can't cry any more. Go ahead and feel lonely. Feel sorry for yourself for a while. Scream and throw a temper tantrum.

Be angry. Be sad. Be grateful. Recognize and deal with all those emotions that come tumbling out.

Why should you let yourself feel all this pain? Otherwise, you will never truly heal. Grief unexpressed does not go away. It lurks just under the surface, waiting to rear its ugly head when you least expect it. Your emotions are less controllable, so you find yourself reacting to things in ways that are entirely out of proportion. You may sob over distant deaths or even cry over a game show. The more you try to hold in all the pain, the more determined it is to come out. You can even make yourself physically sick by refusing to face your grief.

Is it hard to allow the pain? Yes. You may wish to take advantage of a support group so you can share your struggle. Perhaps you prefer to read the stories of others so you gain their wisdom and advice. You may choose quieter activities like writing, playing music, or drawing your experience. You may choose physical activities like sports, running, dancing, or stomping your feet.

It is good to be busy—to have goals and purpose in your life. It is also good to help yourself heal, so you can better enjoy the life you have now. Happiness and satisfaction are still possible, especially if you don't use the busyness of life to avoid doing the things that can help you find them.

Naming the Big White Elephant

Recently, a grieving person reported that she never talks about her loved one who died, her sadness, or her loneliness to any of her friends or family. She does not want to burden them with her troubles or make them feel uncomfortable around her. She doesn't want them to stop inviting her because she isn't "fun" any more. She is afraid—afraid of her emotions being unacceptable, afraid of rejection, and afraid of being left alone.

Unfortunately, even without speaking a word, she is already experiencing all the things she fears. Because she believes that her emotions are unacceptable and that her friends would reject her, she is desperately alone—even in a crowd. No one knows what she is really feeling inside. No one knows her pain. She has to deal with her pain on her own without any resources, help, or support, and she feels isolated and angry at the world because of it.

Do you see yourself in her story? After all, grieving people do make others uncomfortable. People feel helpless around you, unsure what to say or do, and unable to "fix" it.

Grief is often referred to as the elephant in the living room—the enormous creature blocking the path, knocking things over, disrupting everything, and making a big stink every once in a while. Yet, when people come into the living room, they act as if the elephant isn't there. They talk about everything except the elephant. They walk through it or around it. They plug their noses and pretend they don't smell it. Elephants, it seems, are to be ignored. In fact, most people seem too anxious to get back to their own living rooms, where they believe there are no elephants.

Because of all this, those who live with the elephant may start to wonder whether they are crazy. Then, finally, someone who also sees the elephant comes in. What a relief! You mean I'm not crazy? There really is an elephant here? And there are ways to deal with it, to befriend it, and to build a new future? As one bereaved parent said, "I ignore the elephant until I find someone else who also sees it. Then we can really talk."

Few have the patience, skill, and empathy to listen long and, frankly, to avoid giving you unwanted advice and simply walk through the grief with you. Yet don't let that isolate you. Find those friends or family members who can. Take advantage of counseling or grief coaching. Ask around about support groups. You may be amazed at how many other people are also living with big white elephants. Give yourself permission to share your experience so that you do not have to be alone in your grief.

The Changing Palette

John Paul Floyd was six years old—a carefree, loving boy. He was playing with his brother David in the front yard of their home when, without warning, a car jumped the curb and struck the two boys. David was injured, and John Paul was killed. Thus began the nightmare for the Floyd family.

Gregory Floyd, the boys' father, described his grief journey in a wonderful book entitled A Grief Unveiled. He also helped create videos on grief and gave talks and presentations. One of his images for the grief process may be particularly helpful to you.

Greg reported that even in the beginning, when the grief is most intense and the pain is searing, there are sometimes brief moments of joy. Some little thing makes you smile. Someone unexpectedly gives you a hug when you most need it. You momentarily lose yourself in a movie or a show, and you laugh out loud.

Those moments can bring instant guilt. "How can I be happy when this person I love just died?" You may feel you are being disloyal to the person's memory when you don't remain in your grief. You may even feel that you aren't ready to let go of the pain because the pain is your closest connection to the one who died: if the pain is diminishing, perhaps the connection is diminishing.

Yet grieving well does not mean being sad every second of every day. We need those little breaks and rays of sunshine to survive. Greg advised that we should treasure those moments of joy because they sustain us. He called them the "bright splashes of color on the gray palette of grief."

Don't worry. You will neither lose your grief nor forget your loved one if you smile occasionally. Those smiles are the necessary break in the bleakness, the glimmer of hope that perhaps there can still be happiness in life.

As you continue to heal, those "good" times become more frequent and more intense, while the bad times become less frequent and less intense. For instance, one day you realize that you cried only for a half-hour that day. Then you realize you haven't cried in three days. Eventually, you pass the milestone where you haven't cried in weeks. It takes a long time, and the balance shifts back and forth on a regular basis.

Finally, you reach a point where the pain of grief does not define you. Your palette has changed. The joy is no longer the bright splash of color on the gray palette of grief. Instead, the pain becomes the gray splash of color on the bright palette of life.

You never totally lose the gray. You will experience grief bursts or "ambushes" for as long as you live. You will never stop missing the one you so loved or wondering what life would be like if he or she were still alive. Yet you don't have to live your life in gray tones. There is still exuberant color waiting for you, unbridled joy to experience, new things to learn, loving friends to meet, and a promising future to rebuild.

It is a long process to move from a gray palette to a colored one. Start by accepting those splashes of color and treasuring each one as a gift. Allow yourself whatever joy you can without guilt or regret. After all, your best memorial to the ones who died is to live as fully and colorfully as possible, enriched by their memory.

The Fog of Grief: A Widow's Essay

This morning, it was so foggy I could barely see across the street. People appeared out of nowhere, walked by, and disappeared again. Like a scene from a horror movie, it was an uncertain, claustrophobic, potentially dangerous world.

Ah, but then the sun fought through. I can see the old tree, its barren branches framing a plane in the distance. More distant still are wispy clouds. My world now encompasses thousands of people—flying, driving, and working. Everything looks and feels entirely different. Of course, the world has not substantially changed since this morning. It is my perception—the depth and clarity of my vision—that makes it appear so.

Likewise, when my husband died, the world closed in. The sunshine of our dreams was forever shrouded, and my world went gray and cold. I was blinded by pain—by the loss of one I held so dear. I felt cut off, empty, and surrounded by swirling shadows, unable to envision a future.

About six weeks after John's death, I told a friend that my entire future was wiped out in an instant. She said, "No, your future wasn't wiped out. Your husband's was. You still have a future; it will just be a much different future than you had planned."

Her words struck hard. I wasn't allowing myself to see the future because I didn't want it to exist without him. Yet I didn't want to live in a dismal fog for the rest of my life. I did indeed have a future; it was my choice to step into it.

Burning away the fog was hard work and took a long, long time. Slowly, my future emerged from the haze and began taking shape. Eventually, as the light poked through, I stepped tentatively out of the mist, and it felt good.

I know now that the world does not disappear when death occurs. It is only my perception—the depth and clarity of my vision—that makes it seem so. Though the sun may be veiled, it is not extinguished. The future may be shrouded, but it still exists, waiting to be discovered. Life may seem empty, but joy, surprises, and delight yet abound. Beyond the murkiness lie new possibilities, if only we have eyes to see and courage to follow our sight.

The Greatest Gift

Some people run away from grief, go on world cruises or move to another house or another town. But they do not escape, I think. The memories, unbidden, spring into their minds, scattered perhaps over the years, but always there. There is, maybe, something to be said for facing them all deliberately and straightaway...

I would not run away from grief; and I would not try to hold onto it when—if, unbelievably—it passed.

– Sheldon Vanauken, *A Severe Mercy*

It is a universal human experience: when something good happens, we want to remember it. How often have we heard (or said) "I will never forget this day as long as I live" or "I will always remember what you have done for me?" The desire to remember—to immortalize certain people or events—takes on extreme importance when someone you love dies.

I was widowed at the age of twenty-five when my husband John was killed in a car accident. People flooded the wake and funeral, and it was gratifying to know he had made a difference to so many. Still, the rest of the world took no notice. I was appalled as I rode to the cemetery and saw people gardening, buying groceries, and proceeding with their normal routines. I felt that John deserved five minutes of silent prayer, flags lowered to half-mast, schools canceled for the day, or some recognition of his loving, generous life. I instantly understood why survivors build memorials to the deceased.

In the awful time following the funeral, there were many ways to memorialize John. I made dozens of reprints of photographs and distributed them to anyone who was interested. His watch, scrapbook, and other mementos became precious treasures. Because John had worked with the youth in our town, a scholarship fund was started in his name, and enough money was contributed to make a yearly award to a graduating senior. I gave many of John's clothes to family and friends so they could have a visual reminder of him. I kept the rest of his clothes in a special drawer, sometimes wearing one item or just holding it, stroking it, remembering, and crying.

I struggled to conceive of spending my life without John. It made me more determined than ever to remember. I concentrated on his laugh, his eyes, his hands, and his walk. When I couldn't picture a scene with absolute clarity, I panicked. I wanted him to stay "alive," and my mind refused to cooperate. Despite my efforts, he could never again be alive for me. My fuzzy recollections were simply reminders of that fact.

It took much pain and tremendous struggle, but I began to heal. Little by little, I built a life for myself apart from John. Piece by piece, I parted with the clothes that had been so precious. I still have some physical reminders of John, but the ways of remembering that were so important to me in those first two or three years have lost their extreme significance now. I replaced them with new ways of remembering and with a new understanding of what it means to remember.

In its simplest form, remembering means merely "bringing again to mind." As I realized I could no longer bring aspects of John to mind with clarity, I feared that I was forgetting him. Yet there is a deeper meaning to remembering. A "member" is a part of the whole. "Remembering" entails recalling the important aspects and people of my past and assimilating them into my being. My most indelible "memory" of John, then, is not the physical details. The most indelible memory I carry is myself—who I was and who I have become as a result of his influence in my life. Other people were also permanently affected by knowing him. There is no fame, wealth, power, or status in that; yet it is the most important contribution that any of us can make. The world—my world—is a better place because of John.

My lessons did not stop with John's life. His death is undoubtedly the most heart-wrenching, exhausting, and difficult thing that ever happened to me. Yet, as a consequence, I am more compassionate and empathetic. I have a clearer sense of my strengths and weaknesses. I am more tolerant of others and their limitations. My faith is stronger and more deeply rooted. I am more appreciative and loving.

I rarely take people, things, or life itself for granted because I am aware in my innermost being of the swiftness with which it can disappear. I am an optimist. I believe in the ultimate goodness of life and in the power of joint human and divine effort to transform senseless tragedy into blessing. The grief experience has changed the way I live, and the changes have been positive.

I remember feeling that I would never be truly happy again. Thankfully, I was wrong. I am happy now, delighted with life and living it vibrantly. I have been to hell and back, I was transformed by my experience, and I am better for it. That is a memory worth hanging on to.

Twelve Steps for Healthy Grieving

You never thought it would happen to you. Yet here you are, grieving and in pain. It is so tempting to ignore the emotions of grief because they hurt so deeply. Yet unresolved grief is like buried toxic waste: although it isn't evident on the surface, it keeps finding ways to come up, often with unpleasant consequences. It may manifest as headaches or stomachaches, as outbursts of anger or impatience against people who don't deserve it, as depression or suicidal thoughts, or as paranoia or withdrawal from life. It may make you reluctant to get close to another person, or it may make you afraid to love.

The truth is this: Nothing can simply make your grief go away. You must acknowledge, face, and resolve your grief.

This list of suggestions for healthy ways to cope with grief may be helpful as you follow your own path to healing.

1. Expect to recover. Affirm that you will be able to make it and that the resources you need are there if you want them.

2. Set long-range goals for things you eventually would like to have or do. Allow yourself to dream, even if it seems crazy.

3. Do short-term things: go to a movie, soak in a bath, read a good book—whatever comforts you and brings some relief.

4. Never go to sleep without breathing deeply, smiling at least once, and being thankful for what you still have.

5. Keep in touch with your feelings as you ride the roller coaster of up and down, round and round, and back and forth. All grief gets "reworked." You go through it repeatedly, yet you are always moving forward.

6. Find ways to express your emotions. Write in a private journal, pound nails into wood, paint, sculpt, throw a tennis ball against a wall vigorously, write a letter to the one who died or left you, and do what seems right with it (e.g., bury it at the gravesite, tear it up, burn it, keep it in a memory box, etc.).

7. Find at least one person you can talk to honestly and from the heart. If possible, also find a good support group.

8. Read as much as you can. There is great wisdom in the experience of others.

9. Ask for and give forgiveness, whether to the person who died, God, or those still living. None of us are perfect people; we are just people. Accept your imperfections and limitations, and be willing to ask forgiveness for whatever you feel you did wrong or for whatever you feel you didn't do. Work through the experiences of hurt and anger until you can offer forgiveness in return. Lack of forgiveness shackles your heart, mind, and body. Forgiveness sets you free.

10. Remember the past, fondly and often, but don't live in the past. There is no future in that.

11. Decide you want to heal. Some people can't let go of the pain, whether from a sense of misplaced loyalty, fear of living without it, or unwillingness to build a new future. Decide that whatever life you have left is still well worth living. Decide to look for joy. Decide to make each day as good as possible.

12. Make others smile. Give of yourself. Live in such a way that when you die, the world will be a better place because you lived.

Where Do I Turn?
Recommended Books on Grief and Loss

Giving clients a good book is a highly effective way to offer them consolation, reliable advice, and solid information. They appreciate your thoughtfulness, especially if the book is closely matched to their own situation. Yet you do not have time to research the array of books that are available so you know what to give. We've done the work for you.

Here you find titles and descriptions of books about grief covering a range of styles and organized into situational categories. Some are recent, most were published within the last ten to fifteen years, and a few are old workhorses, published long ago but still well worth reading.

Often, newly bereaved people lack the concentration and desire to read long or complex books, so several listings consist of short chapters in easy-to-read formats. There are also more substantial books, for those who want information immediately or for those past the initial stages of grief who seek greater understanding.

We've noted when a book is spiritual or religious and where a clear denominational focus exists. In the absence of such comments, assume the book is secular in nature.

It's impossible to include every worthy book in this list. We base selections on our own reading, book reviews, personal experience, and over twenty-five years of working in the field of bereavement. Yet this list is fluid and change-able. You may wish to add to it yourself by asking clients for the names of books they found help-ful when they were grieving.

If you need resources for a situation not listed here, or if you need more specific advice, please e-mail us at hello@corgenius.com.

Also, e-mail to let us know which books your clients find particularly pertinent or if you feel a book should be deleted from the list. We're always interested in the feedback of others whose experiences are different from ours so we can improve our offerings.

Before a Death Occurs

1. Morris, Virginia. *Talking about death won't kill you.* Workman Publishing, 2001.

   Many people find it difficult to talk in specifics about their wishes for treatment as they approach death, disposition of the body, last rites, etc. This book gets the conversation going in easy, comfortable ways.

2. Callanan, Maggie and Patricia Kelley. *Final Gifts: Understanding the Special Awareness, Needs, and Communications of the Dying.* Simon and Schuster, 2012. (Updated from the 1997 version)

   This book ought to be on every shelf. In clear and simple terms, these two hospice nurses tell story after story to illustrate the ways we can understand what loved ones experience as they die. It lets family members truly communicate with their dying loved one, finish unfinished business, and help achieve the kind of peaceful death everyone hopes to have.

   Recommended for anyone with aging parents, family members who are frequently ill, the family of a terminally ill patient, and all those wanting to make the death process easier for everyone involved.

3. Wooten-Green, Ron. *When the Dying Speak.* Loyola Press, 2001

   The author is a hospice chaplain, a former university professor, and a widower himself. Drawing on his personal and ministerial experiences and writing from a Christian perspective, he uses each chapter to explain elements of communicating with dying people and then concludes with reflection questions for the reader.

   Recommended for people from Christian faith traditions who want to be truly present during the dying process of a beloved person

General Grief

4. Davidson, Judy. *Grieving Well: A personal journal for adults about loss.* Center for Personal Recovery, 2002.

   The author was widowed at thirty and then survived the death of her oldest son when he was seventeen. As a grief educator and counselor, she skillfully created this interactive journal to help adults coping with the death of a loved one. Journaling is a well-established coping and healing mechanism, and Davidson's gentle leading questions make it comfortable to write about unresolved relationship issues, difficult days, positive memories, and new life.

   Recommended for any adult coping with the death of a loved one

5. Peter McWilliams, Harold Bloomfield and Melba Colgrove. H*ow to Survive the Loss of a Love.* Prelude Press, 1993.

   Grieving people are overwhelmed on many emotional and physical levels, and they appreciate smaller doses of information, support, and encouragement. This book is full of brief messages, including practical suggestions, proverbs, reminders, advice, and more. Readers can open the book randomly and find comfort on virtually every page.

   Recommended for anyone after death, divorce, estrangement, abandonment, or loss of a significant relationship

6. Johnson, Joy and Marvin Johnson. *What It Is and What You Can Do.* Centering Corp, 1995.

   This inexpensive, small pamphlet contains user-friendly definitions and helpful hints. It is a brief, easy-to-read overview of grief appropriate for immediately after a death.

Recommended for people in the initial stages who would never tackle a whole book

7. Rando, Therese. *How to Go On Living When Someone You Love Dies.* Bantam, 1988.

Rando is a clinical psychologist and one of the most respected authors on bereavement for professional and personal audiences. She packed this book with well-researched information, advice, and resources for anyone who grieves. It is informative, compassionate, and down-to-earth.

Recommended for anyone grieving the death of a loved one, whether the death was last week or last year

8. Grollman, Earl. *Living When a Loved One Has Died.* Beacon Press, 1997.

The author wrote this longtime friend of the bereaved more than twenty years ago. This short book endures because it's easy to read and understand during the initial confusion of bereavement, yet it offers helpful words of comfort and guidance.

Recommended during the initial stages of grief or as an easy read at any point in the process

9. Grollman, Earl. *What Helped Me When My Loved One Died.* Beacon Press, 1982.

Rather than writing this book himself, Grollman assembled the stories of bereaved people and let them tell, in their own words, what helped them most when they were grieving. It is insightful and touching.

Recommended especially during the first six months to a year after a death and for those who live or work with bereaved people

10. Golden, Thomas R. *Swallowed by a Snake: The Gift of the Masculine Side of Healing.* Golden Healing Publishing, 1996.

Much grief therapy is aimed toward the traditionally "feminine" tasks of reflection, relationships, and sharing of pain. Golden wrote this book to blend those tasks with the more traditionally "male" coping mechanisms of action, logic, and practicality. He found that both men and women have a blend of these characteristics, an insight that was confirmed by later research on grieving styles (referenced earlier in this guide). This book, then, is a useful, balanced resource for any grieving adult.

Recommended for anyone who wants to understand our society's long-standing assumptions and be freed to grieve in his or her own style

11. Attig, Thomas. *How We Grieve: Relearning the World.* Oxford University Press, 2011.

The author recently revised this classic book, as he continues to draw on his thirty years of teaching and counseling. His core understanding is that grieving requires fundamentally "relearning the world" at every level. In this book, he offers rich stories, pertinent observations, and thoughtful reflections. His is a more objective look at grief that is well worth the read.

Recommended for anyone wanting to better understand the process of grief, whether they're currently grieving, anticipating a loss, or supporting a grieving person

12. Kushner, Harold. *When Bad Things Happen to Good People.* Schocken, 1981.

This Jewish rabbi writes for people of any Judeo-Christian faith tradition as he fearlessly addresses the dilemma created by the existence of suffering when God is supposed to be so good. This is a persuasive and hopeful examination of the empty platitudes often offered to the bereaved, and it poses a challenge to embrace the doubts, questions, and ambiguities of faith in the midst of crisis, death, and grief.

Recommended for those experiencing anger toward God or a faith crisis because of suffering or death

13. Elison, Jennifer and Chris McGonigle. *Liberating Losses: When Death Brings Relief*. Da Capo Press, 2004.

When a person dies, his or her loved one is expected to grieve. What happens if the primary emotion is relief? For instance, a dying loved one may be trapped in an increasingly debilitated body, and death is a longed-for release. Perhaps the person struggled with alcoholism or addiction and wreaked havoc in the family. Regardless of the cause, experiencing relief when someone dies is often a trigger for guilt. This honest yet compassionate book contains personal stories and case histories that validate the emotion most grieving people feel obliged to hide.

Recommended for "relieved grievers": those in circumstances where relief is a significant component of the grief process

14. Noel, Brook & Pamela D. Blair. *I Wasn't Ready to Say Goodbye: Surviving, Coping, and Healing after the Sudden Death of a Loved One.* Champion Press, 2000.

Full of information for survivors of sudden death, this book begins by offering advice on calls to make, planning the service, and handling other immediate concerns. It goes on through the grief process, allowing for

differences of age, gender, and relationship to the deceased.

Recommended any time from the initial notification of a sudden death through the grief process

15. Sanders, Catherine M. *Surviving Grief... and Learning to Live Again.* John Wiley & Sons, 1992.

This author received the 1990 award for Outstanding Contribution in the Field of Death-Related Counseling. Her expertise shows as she blends extensive research, numerous interviews, and personal experience into the foundation of this book. By examining different situations, Sanders encourages readers to learn about and experience the grief process with its emotions, reactions, and expectations and to move toward healing.

Recommended for anyone who grieves

16. Smith, Harold Ivan. *Grieving the Death of a Friend.* Augsburg Fortress, 1996.

Though these stories, quotes, and insights focus on close friendships and our society's denial of "friend grief," the wisdom they contain is helpful for anyone who grieves. The reflections begin with the dying process and continue through burying, mourning, remembering and reconciling. Finally, Smith includes rituals and suggestions for healing.

Recommended for anyone who grieves, but it is especially helpful during and after the death of a beloved person who wasn't an immediate family member

17. Westberg, Granger E. *Good Grief.* Minneapolis: Fortress, 1997.

Originally written nearly forty years ago, this little book is still widely used. Westberg, drawing on extensive experience as a minister and counselor, demonstrates his belief that our response to smaller grief experiences affects our response to larger losses. He describes ten "stages" common to grief and shows how each one can bring growth and healing.

An old classic, recommended for anyone who grieves, particularly in the early stages when concentration is limited

18. Sittser, Gerald. *Grace Disguised: How the Soul Grows Through Loss.* Zondervan, 1996.

Sittser grapples with senseless tragedy and unexplainable loss after a drunk driver slams into a car, killing his mother, his wife of twenty-four years, and his four-year-old daughter. Although employed as a religion professor, he struggles with questions of faith, coming only at long last to peace with God. This book is powerful.

Recommended for Christians dealing with sudden, tragic, or multiple deaths

19. Wolfelt, Alan D. *Understanding Your Grief: Ten Essential Touchstones for Finding Hope and Healing Your Heart.* Companion Press, 2004.

The author, director of the Center for Loss and Life Transition, discusses factors that make grief unique for each person, describes what people normally think and feel during the grief process, and offers advice about how to get through it and heal. The book includes journaling sections that allow readers to formulate their thoughts in writing (a helpful strategy).

Recommended for those in any stage of the grief process

20. Doka, Kenneth J. *Living with Grief: After Sudden Loss, Suicide, Homicide, Accident, Heart Attack, Stroke.* Taylor and Francis, 1996.

Written by a preeminent researcher and therapist in the field of grief, this is an honest, valuable book for family members grieving sudden and unexpected death. In addition to the situations listed in the title, there is a helpful discussion of surviving the death of those in the military.

Recommended for those grieving a sudden, unexpected, or traumatic death, including military death

Death of a Spouse

21. Sieden, Othniel J. & Jane L. Bilett. *When Your Spouse Dies — A Widow & Widower's Handbook.* Books to Believe In, 2008.

The co-authors are a medical doctor who was widowed and a psychologist who eventually became his wife. They discuss financial issues and practical concerns while outlining an emotional road map to help guide widows and widowers as they heal and rebuild their lives.

Recommended for widowed people from the time of the death through the grief process

22. Curry, Cathleen L. *When Your Spouse Dies: A Concise and Practical Source of Help and Advice.* Notre Dame: Ave Maria Press, 1990.

Widowed at the age of forty-seven with nine children to raise (her husband had a massive heart attack on the day before Father's Day), Curry incorporates her own experience and establishes eight practical guideposts for getting through the first year. She deals with topics ranging from expressions of mourning and caring for one's own health to loneliness, anger, sexuality, and financial planning. She emphasizes spiritual growth as essential to healing. This useful book is currently in its sixth printing.

Recommended for widowed persons, especially those who are younger and have children

23. Ginsburg, Genevieve Davis. *Widow to Widow: Thoughtful, Practical Ideas for Rebuilding your Life.* Fisher Books, 1995.

Ginsburg is the founder of Widowed to Widowed Services, and she writes frankly and honestly about the needs, questions, and concerns of the widowed (men and women). She covers everything from emptying his or her closet, to traveling and eating alone, to money matters, to dating and sexuality. This is a wise, useful guide.

Recommended for any widowed person at any time

24. Ericcson, Stephanie. *Companion through the Darkness: Inner Dialogues on Grief.* HarperCollins, 1993.

The author began keeping a journal after her husband died while she was pregnant with their only child. She combines excerpts from that journal with brief essays, capturing the raw, wrenching depth of the emotions involved in grief.

Recommended for young widows, especially soon after the death

25. Brothers, Joyce. *Widowed.* Ballatine Publishing, 1990.

This is the personal story of a psychologist who thought she knew all there was to know about grieving a spouse's death until her own husband of thirty years died. It is wonderfully well written and serves as a comprehensive, down-to-earth, sometimes humorous, compassionate, and gentle look at the difficulties of negotiating the grief process as a widow.

Recommended for any widowed person

26. Campbell, Scott & Phyllis R. Silverman. *Widower: When Men are Left Alone.* Baywood, 1995.

A journalist and a behavioral scientist do a remarkable job of capturing the range of situations and emotions men feel when a wife dies. Each chapter centers on one widower. The authors give a brief biography and then allow the subject himself to tell his story and feelings in his own words. They follow this with well-done commentary grounded in research, pointing out aspects of each story that are important. It is a helpful, informative, and refreshing resource.

Recommended for men who are widowed

27. Feinberg, Linda. *I'm Grieving as Fast as I Can.* New Horizon Press, 1994.

Largely told through the stories of clients and friends combined with her own experience, Feinberg writes for young widows and widowers, often with small children. They immediately face issues of dating and sexuality, feel the burden of the family's needs, and struggle with the sense of a stolen or empty future. The author sensitively covers issues relating to a relationship that was stormy or abusive and even the loss of a fiancé.

Recommended for those under fifty who are widowed

28. Felber, Marta. *Finding Your Way after Your Spouse Dies*. Notre Dame: Ave Maria Press, 2000.

Having been through the experience, Felber offers sixty-four one-page essays on aspects of the grief process, from embracing loneliness, to reliving the day of the death, to dealing with guilt, and more. A brief Christian prayer and two scripture suggestions follow each essay. The book is practical, inspirational, honest, and easy to read.

Recommended for Christians who are widowed, especially those in the early stages of grief

29. Zonnebelt-Smeenge, Susan J. & Robert C. De Vries. *Getting to the Other Side of Grief*. Baker Books, 1998.

A female clinical psychologist and a male pastor, each of whom was widowed, wrote this unique book for the widowed. Written from a Christian perspective, it presents a compassionate challenge to work out grief without avoidance, using insights for the different ways in which men and women deal with a spouse's death.

Recommended for widowed persons regardless of gender or grieving style

Parental Death – for Adults

30. Bartocci, Barbara. *Nobody's Child Anymore; Grieving, Caring, and Comforting When Parents Die*. Notre Dame: Sorin Books, 2000.

Through nostalgia, a variety of stories, instruction, and inspiration, Bartocci captures the unique loss and life issues that accompany the death of a parent for an adult child. Unlike most grief books, she starts with the dying process and then

goes on to issues of grieving, caring for the surviving parent, and healing from the loss. It is a wonderfully written, touching book, helpful to anyone who is grieving a parent's death.

Recommended from the time of a parent's terminal diagnosis through the death and grief

31. Akner, Lois F. *How to Survive the Loss of a Parent: A Guide for Adults*. Morrow, 1993.

This book duplicates the setting of an actual ongoing workshop for adults whose parent(s) have died. There are twelve participants reflecting a range of ages, social and religious backgrounds, and family structure. In this informal format, the author (a psychotherapist) deftly guides the reader through the issues and emotions of parent loss in an accessible, sensible way.

Recommended for anyone whose parent dies

32. Myers, Edward. *When Parents Die: A Guide for Adults*. Penguin, 1997.

This book includes thoughtful advice from therapists, first-person accounts, and a detailed description of the author's own experience when each of his parents died. Myers knows how devastating a parent's death is, no matter how old you are. He covers the differences between sudden death and slow decline; gives advice for funerals, dividing property, and dealing with practical matters; and addresses resolving feelings of guilt, shame, and unfinished business.

Recommended from the time of a parent's diagnosis or death through the first six to nine months after the death

33. Chethik, Neil. *Fatherloss: How Sons of All Ages Come to Terms with the Deaths of Their Dads.* Hyperion, 2001.

This extraordinary book is based on a landmark national survey of more than 300 men whose fathers died plus extended interviews with seventy others. It details how men react differently to a father's death at ages ranging from childhood, young adulthood, to middle age and older and then discusses what helps most.

Recommended highly for any man whose father died, even if the death was years ago

34. Smith, Harold Ivan. *On Grieving the Death of a Father.* Augsburg Fortress, 1994.

Smith is a prolific author on grief who intertwines his own experience with wisdom from the ages, such as Frederick Buechner, Norman Vincent Peale, Corrie ten Boom, and many other recognizable people. This easy read offers tidbits of wisdom to help heal without delving deeply into trauma.

Recommended soon after the death for middle-aged or older men whose father has died

35. Smith, Harold Ivan. *Grieving the Death of a Mother.* Augsburg Fortress, 2003.

The same author who almost ten years earlier wrote about the death of his father now writes an accessible and thorough book about the death of mothers. He describes his own experience but includes the experiences of many other people whose lives were deeply affected when their mother died. He begins his story with the dying process and continues through ways to remember and honor a mother long after her death.

Recommended for adult children from the time of their mother's terminal diagnosis through the grieving process

36. Ainley, Rosa, ed. *Death of a Mother: Daughters' Stories.* HarperCollins, 1991.

This is a wonderful collection of more than thirty pieces written by women about the deaths of their mothers. Some are funny, others are filled with rage, some are despairing, and others are full of love. Well-known authors write some stories, while other authors are everyday women. The pieces include poetry, prose, reflection, and narrative.

Recommended for any woman whose mother has died

37. Simon, Clea. *Fatherless Women: How We Change After We Lose Our Dads.* John Wiley & Sons, 2001.

This highly acclaimed author and Boston Globe columnist fills her book with moving stories of real women combined with her own experience of her father's death. In some cases, the contributor's relationship with her father was enviable, and in others, it was conflicted. Regardless, each woman's thoughts contribute insights on making peace with the past and accepting the present, with a goal of moving into the future whole and healed.

Recommended for any woman whose father dies, regardless of the kind of relationship she had with him

38. Edelman, Hope. *Motherless Daughters: the Legacy of Loss.* Da Capo Press, 2006.

In this second edition, Edelman uses the experience of her mother's death when she was seventeen along with interviews of hundreds of other women whose mothers died, disappeared, or were otherwise lost from their lives. Combined with solid research, she explores the implications of yearning for the absent mother on a woman's self-concept, esteem, identity, and future relationships.

Recommended particularly for young adult women whose mother is absent through death, separation, or abandonment

Child Death – for Parents or Siblings

39. Rosenblatt, Paul C. *Help Your Marriage Survive the Death of a Child.* Philadelphia: Temple University Press, 2000.

A marriage requires hard work at the best of times. The impact of the death of a child can tear a family and marriage to shreds as the couple shuts down, turns away, or moves inward. Rosenblatt includes helpful information on how people grieve individually and in relationships; the impact of grief on sexuality; dealing with friends, relatives, and co-workers; the frequency of depression; and other important issues.

Recommended for couples at any time following a child's death

40. Davis, Deborah. *Empty Cradle, Broken Heart: Surviving the Death of Your Baby.* Fulcrum Publishing, 1991.

This is a wonderful, comforting book for parents grieving the death of a baby—miscarriage, stillborn, shortly after birth, or within the first year of life. The combination of personal narrative, research, and inspiration makes this a valuable resource. One unique aspect of the book is that it doesn't have to be read front to back; instead, it allows parents to choose topics specific to their situations.

Recommended in the initial stages of grief for any couple whose baby died before or after birth

41. Arnold, Joan Hagan & Penelope Buschman Gemma. *A Child Dies: A Portrait of Family Grief.* The Charles Press, 1994.

Two nurses have written a comprehensive, invaluable resource for families struggling with the death of a child, whether it's an infant, a toddler, or an older child. The authors include powerful art and touching poetry along with practical advice from understanding companions.

Recommended for any couple or family grieving a child's death

42. McCracken, Anne & Mary Semel. *A Broken Heart Still Beats After Your Child Dies.* Hazelden, 1998.

This partnership of a social worker and a journalist, both of whom experienced the death of a child, results in a remarkable collection of poetry, fiction, and essays that indirectly but effectively capture the profound grief of parents when their child dies.

Recommended for parents any time after a still-at-home child dies

43. Westerhoff, Nicholas. *Lament for a Son.* Eerdmans, 1987.

In this powerfully written book, Wolterstorff (a professor of philosophical theology at Yale) grapples with questions, doubts, and family grief after his twenty-five-year-old son's death in a skiing accident. He incorporates philosophy, scripture, and poetry, and the afterword is a requiem written in memory of his son that was performed in Grand Rapids, Michigan.

Recommended for those with a slightly more academic or literary bent, especially within the first year

44. Wezeman, Phyllis Vos & Kenneth R. Wezeman. *Finding Your Way after Your Child Dies.* Ave Maria Press, 2001.

This book is a touching guide that helps parents acknowledge and deal with their feelings. It includes fifty-two themes, ranging from birthdays to graduation, and other events that may happen daily, weekly, or just once. Each theme includes a story or teaching about an aspect of grief, practical activities and rituals for coping, a reading from scripture, and a Christian prayer.

Recommended especially for Christian parents whose deceased child was under the age of eighteen

45. Wray, T.J. *Surviving the Death of a Sibling: Living Through Grief When an Adult Brother or Sister Dies.* Three Rivers Press, 2003.

This collection of stories by the author and many other sibling grievers is an excellent resource. The book is comforting, challenging, and inspiring while giving practical steps a grieving person can take to cope with a sibling's death.

Recommended for anyone over eighteen whose sibling dies

46. Berman, Claire. *When a Brother or Sister Dies: Looking Back, Moving Forward.* Praeger Publishers, 2009.

The author, whose adult sister died of a heart illness, takes an honest look at the fact that attention tends to focus on the grief of parents or children of the deceased rather than the grief of siblings. She admits the intense mix of emotions accompanying a

sibling's death in light of the shared identity, intimate family history, and sometimes competitive or conflicted relationships that are common within families, and offers compassion and advice to survivors.

Recommended to adults surviving the death of a sibling

47. Donnelly, Katherine Fair. *Recovering From the Loss of a Sibling: When a Brother or Sister Dies.* Universe, 2000.

Numerous testimonials from surviving siblings of all ages form the foundation of this book. It addresses the unique grief of siblings and the fact that siblings are often overlooked in the outpouring of support for parents. The book is insightful and comforting.

Recommended for siblings from age ten to adult

48. Richter, Elizabeth. *Losing Someone You Love: When a Brother or Sister Dies.* Putnam, 1986.

This book consists of fifteen stories written by ten- to nineteen-year-olds whose brother or sister died. The cause of death varies widely: accidents, suicide, murder, disease, and even sudden infant death syndrome (SIDS). These honest stories let teens know they're not alone in their grief and that they will survive and heal.

Recommended for teens after a sibling dies

49. Barber, Erika R. *Letters From a Friend: A Sibling's Guide for Coping and Grief.* Baywood, 2003.

This unique workbook includes therapeutic activities addressing the needs of children and adolescents after a sibling's death. It is organized into four sections: hospitalization, illness, injury, and death. Readers can easily remove pages to allow personalization of the text. This also allows independent use, so children and teens can create a personal journal of their bereavement and a chronicle of their lives as surviving siblings. It can be used by the entire family and/or in conjunction with a professional therapist.

Recommended for children or teens any time from a sibling's serious illness through death and the grieving process

50. Wittberger, Patricia & Russ Wittberger. *When a Child Dies from Drugs: Practical Help for Parents in Bereavement.* Xlibris Corporation, 2004.

This book is by and for parents whose child dies from drugs or alcohol. It is also a useful guide for those who want to effectively support the grieving parents. It delves into the pain and stigma but also offers hope and practical advice.

Recommended for family and friends who survive a death caused by alcohol or drugs and for those who want to support them

51. Strommen, Merton & A. Irene Strommen. *Five Cries of Grief: One Family's Journey to Healing After the Tragic Death of a Son.* Minneapolis: Augsburg, 1996.

This couple chronicles their grief journey following their twenty-five-year-old son's death from a lightning strike. One unique aspect is that each author tells the story from their own perspective, highlighting the differences in each one's reactions and timetables and acknowledging the absolute necessity of accepting and dealing with those differences. They also reinforce the timeless aspect of grief and note that no magical healing occurs by the time of the anniversary.

Recommended for anyone in grief, but especially for couples and families grieving together

Books For and About Children or Teens

52. Grollman, Earl A. *Straight Talk About Death for Teenagers: How to Cope with Losing Someone You Love.* Boston: Beacon Press, 1994.

Earl Grollman has written more than twenty books on grief. This book uses an informal and accessible style to guide often-forgotten teenagers through the grieving process. Grollman doesn't go into depth on topics, and some may feel he glosses over too much. That is wise because teens aren't going to pick up a tome on grief. They will read this kind of introductory resource.

Recommended highly for teenagers who are grieving

53. Fitzgerald, Helen. *The Grieving Teen: A Guide for Teenagers and Their Friends.* Fireside, 2000.

In a clear, accessible way, Fitzgerald guides teens from the sickbed to the funeral, and from the first day back at school to the first anniversary of the death. She adeptly covers the entire range of situations for teen grief, helping them address the intense emotions they face as they deal with grief and adolescence simultaneously.

Recommended highly for teenagers coping with death

54. Davidson, Judy. *Grief Skills for Life: A Personal Journal for Teens About Loss.* Center for Personal Recovery, 2002.

Davidson is a death educator and trauma specialist whose oldest son died in a car accident at seventeen. This book is an interactive journal, inviting teens to write, draw, and color so they can laugh, cry, and release their emotions. It is cathartic, honest, and usable.

Recommended for any teen grieving a death

55. Grollman, Earl & Joy Johnson. *A Child's Book About Death*. Omaha: Centering Corporation, 2001.

This is a brief, easy-to-read, comforting book for children when they face death. It explains death through analogy and experiences that children understand. Adults should spend time with it too.

Recommended for parents and young children whenever death touches a family

56. Markell, Kathryn A. & Marc A. Markell. *The Children Who Lived: Using Harry Potter and Other Fictional Characters to Help Grieving Children and Adolescents*. Routledge, 2008.

This sister and brother have written a creative, resourceful book that allows adults to use stories to help grieving kids and teens. Drawing from all seven Harry Potter stories plus four other classic works of fiction, the book talks about the loss issues they faced and then offers engaging projects, games, and activities to help youth strengthen their own coping skills. The book includes a CD that provides PowerPoint or JPEG formats for all the worksheets.

Recommended for teachers, counselors, parents, and caregivers who are supporting grieving children

57. Johnson, Joy. *Keys to Helping Children Deal with Death and Grief*. Barron's Educational Press, 1999.

Johnson relates her experiences as a bereavement specialist for over thirty years with a particular interest in children's grief. This book helps parents explain death in ways that kids can comprehend. It also explains a child's grief to parents in ways that allow them to understand and help. Stories and practical advice fill this invaluable, personal, and accessible guide.

Recommended for parents and other adults helping children under the age of thirteen

58. Dougy Center Staff. *35 Ways to Help a Grieving Child*. The Dougy Center for Grieving Children, 1999.

Based on years of experience working directly with grieving kids, this guidebook is immensely practical and helpful. It covers topics from how children of different ages grieve, to providing safe outlets for children to express their emotions, to involving kids in decisions that help them heal. Parents who work through this book with their children will benefit too.

Recommended as a workbook for parents and young to middle-aged children

59. Fitzgerald, Helen. *The Grieving Child: A Parent's Guide*. Simon & Schuster, 1992.

Organized like a book on infant care, this book provides practical advice for parents and others caring for bereaved children. The last chapter addresses the unresolved childhood grief that many adults carry and suggests how they can use the book to resolve their own grief while helping their children.

Recommended highly for parents of children from toddler to teenager

60. Huntley, Theresa M. *Helping Children Grieve When Someone They Love Dies*. Minneapolis: Augsburg, 2002.

Huntley brings her energy and expertise as a pediatric nurse to this fine book to help parents (and other adults) to be more intentionally present with grieving children. This book inspires, educates, and motivates. The first and largest section of the book deals with information and advice to help children grieve the death of a loved one. The last third of the book covers how to help and support children who are dying.

Recommended for parents of dying or grieving children from youth through teen years

61. Silverman, Janis. *Help Me Say Goodbye: Activities for Helping Kids Cope When a Special Person Dies*. Fairview Press, 1999.

This little workbook is especially useful for younger children or any grieving children who have difficulty verbalizing their sadness and confusion. The child works through a series of activities, most of them nonverbal, to draw out their inner feelings. It can be equally helpful for the parents who work through it with them.

Recommended highly for young children and their parents

62. Goldman, Linda. *Great Answers to Difficult Questions About Death: What Children Need to Know*. Philadelphia: Jessica Kingsley, 2009.

Adults often wonder how to explain death to children. The author is a licensed counselor and teacher who uses simple sketches, discussion, quotes, questions, tasks, and connections to many resources in this useful guide. Chapters are devoted to religious beliefs, terminal illness, emotions, reactions of others, and the most common questions that kids ask.

Recommended for parents, teachers, youth ministers, and anyone who works with grieving children

Divorce

63. Warren, Sally & Andrea Thompson. *Dumped: A Survival Guide for the Woman Who's Been Left by the Man She Loved*. Avon, 1999.

The authors draw on the experiences of over 100 women whose husbands left them, many times for another woman. The book is a down-to-earth, easy read with plenty of tips for daily survival (including how to answer the "What happened?" question) as well as long-term coping strategies. Warren went through the experience herself, and Thompson has written extensively for women's magazines. Their collaborative effort is one that many women find supportive and helpful.

Recommended for women whose husbands left the marriage

64. Sapphire, Peggy, ed. *The Disenfranchised: Stories of Life and Grief When an Ex-Spouse Dies*. Baywood, 2013.

A counselor who has worked with divorced people extensively collected this anthology of stories. She noticed that, contrary to what many people expect, divorced people can experience profound grief when an ex-spouse dies. This unique resource addresses a common situation that often is not sufficiently validated.

Recommended for divorced people when an ex-spouse dies

65. Fisher, Bruce. *Rebuilding: When Your Relationship Ends.* San Luis: Impact, 2005.

This is a wise, compassionate, and thorough exploration of nineteen building blocks that compose the divorce adjustment process. Each chapter ends with reflective questions and includes child adjustment considerations. Chapters are organized developmentally and include denial, fear, adaptation, loneliness, friendship, guilt/rejection, grief, anger, letting go, self-worth, transition, openness, love, trust, relatedness, sexuality, singleness, purpose, and freedom.

If I had to recommend just one book on divorce adjustment, this would be it

66. Ahrons, Constance. *The Good Divorce: Keeping Your Family Together When Your Marriage Comes Apart.* N.Y: Harper Perennial, 1994.

The author interviewed ninety-eight families over a five-year period. Half of the couples were amicably divorced (cooperative colleagues and perfect pals), and half were enemies (fiery foes and angry associates). Ahrons challenges negative myths and stereotypes of divorce, providing a more accurate description based on the experience of real people. The best part of the book is the author's descriptions of the emotional divorce that precedes the legal divorce.

Recommended for anyone considering, going through, or completing a divorce

67. Margulies, Sam. *Getting Divorced Without Ruining Your Life: A Reasoned, Practical Guide to the Legal, Emotional and Financial Ins and outs of Negotiating a Divorce Settlement.* NY: Fireside, 2001

The author is a lawyer and mediator with two decades of experience who gives extensive information about the legal, financial, and emotional dimensions of divorce. Partners are encouraged to collaborate rather than allow the process to be controlled by lawyers or an adversarial court system. Though by its nature the divorce process is emotionally charged, partners are repeatedly advised to feel but not act out their emotions, to keep their needs (and those of the children) in focus, to avoid being caught in the blame and victim role, and to take responsibility for ongoing choices.

Recommended for couples who have decided to divorce

68. Ricketts, Percy. *Adjusting to Divorce: Simple Steps Parents Can Take to Help Themselves and Their Children.* CreateSpace, 2009.

A psychotherapist and professor whose parenting classes are required for divorcing parents in the state of Florida, Dr. Ricketts highlights seven steps that help parents and their children adjust to the trauma and pain that occur with divorce.

Recommended for any divorcing family with children, especially children between the ages of five and eighteen

69. Nichols, J. Randall. *Ending Marriage, Keeping Faith.* NY: Crossroad, 1993.

The author is a minister and marriage and family therapist who experienced his own divorce. The book deals with the grief process and loss issues and presents an excellent, five-stage model of divorce while addressing questions of faith and religion inherent in the topic.

Recommended for pre- or post-divorce partners struggling with religious and spiritual dimensions of divorce

Dementia

70. National Institute on Aging. *Understanding Memory Loss: Loss: What to Do When You Have Trouble Remembering.*

This free government resource is an invaluable educational tool covering sources of forgetfulness and essential knowledge about dementia. It is available in printable PDF form or for ordering at http://www.nia.nih.gov/alzheimers/publication/understanding-memory-loss.

Recommended for everyone before there are signs of dementia so they understand signs and causes

71. National Institute on Aging. *Caring for a Person with Alzheimer's Disease.*

A more substantial free government booklet, this piece focuses on how a family can best support and access services for someone diagnosed with Alzheimer's. It is available in printable PDF form or for ordering at http://www.nia.nih.gov/alzheimers/publication/caring-for-a-person-with-alzheimers-disease

Recommended for family and caregivers of anyone diagnosed with Alzheimer's disease or other sources of dementia

72. Boss, Pauline. *Loving Someone Who Has Dementia: How to Find Hope While Coping with Stress and Grief.* Jossey-Bass, 2011.

This book isn't so much about the person who has dementia; instead, it's about the caregivers and family members. The author is a therapist who also worked as a professor at the University of Minnesota and at Harvard Medical School. She sensitively discusses how relationships change as dementia progresses and offers seven

guidelines to help caregivers keep their sanity. This is a great resource.

Recommended for the family members, friends, and other concerned people who are dealing with the progressing dementia of a loved one

73. Rubinstein, Nataly. *Alzheimer's Disease and Other Dementias: The Caregiver's Complete Survival Guide.* Two Harbors Press, 2011.

The author is a licensed clinical social worker and certified geriatric care manager specializing in dementia. She worked with dementia patients for two decades and served as her mother's caregiver for sixteen years as her dementia progressed. She draws on her experience of what works and what doesn't, especially in common problem areas, to offer eminently practical, how-to tips for the family members and caregivers. Having navigated the system repeatedly on behalf of others, she includes tips on getting the legal, financial, and medical help you and your loved one need along with a wealth of other information.

Recommended for anyone concerned about or caring for a person with dementia

74. Mace, Nancy L. & Peter V. Rabins. *The 36-Hour Day: A Family Guide to Caring for People Who Have Alzheimer Disease, Related Dementias, and Memory Loss.* John Hopkins University Press, 2011.

Originally published by Johns Hopkins in 1981, this book has been continually revised, updated, and improved and is now in its fifth edition. A valuable and comprehensive manual recommended by the Journal of the American Medical Association, the book covers issues from the causes and prevention of dementia, through handling the early stages, and on to finding appropriate care that manages more advanced dementia.

Recommended as an educational resource for anyone seeking education while facing the possibility or reality of dementia

75. Coste, Joanne Koenig. *Learning to Speak Alzheimer's: A Groundbreaking Approach for Everyone Dealing with the Disease.* Mariner Books, 2004.

The author is an Alzheimer's family therapist and board member of the *American Journal of Alzheimer's Disease & Other Dementias* who raised four children while caring for her husband following his stroke and progressive memory loss. She developed a process she calls "habilitation" to enhance the person's remaining functions while compensating for what they have lost and to improve the level of communication between all concerned. She doesn't offer education about the illness itself and assumes a full-time caregiver relationship. In that context, she offers useful advice and tips on a wide range of issues (e.g., recipes for nutritious finger foods and helping the person get a good night's sleep). This is a highly regarded source of information from a nationally recognized expert.

Recommended for people who want input on emotional and personal aspects of caring for their loved one with dementia, particularly if they are full-time caregivers

76. Miller, Mark D. & Charles F. Reynolds III. *Depression and Anxiety in Later Life: What Everyone Needs to Know.* Johns Hopkins Press, 2012.

Millions of elderly people struggle with depression and anxiety, often complicated by memory problems, health issues, physical pain, difficulty eating or sleeping, and end-of-life fears. This book delves into the causes, symptoms, and treatments of mental disorders in older people. The aim is to help the elderly, their family members, and caregivers identify symptoms and make positive lifestyle changes to help the "golden years" have a little more luster.

Recommended for aging people, their adult children, and caregivers

Death by Suicide

77. Fine, Carla. *No Time to Say Goodbye: Surviving the Suicide of a Loved One.* Three Rivers Press, 1999; Kindle, 2011

The author's husband of twenty-one years was a successful physician at the top of his game when he killed himself. Feeling stunned, stigmatized, guilty, isolated, and at a loss for resources, she wrote this comprehensive manual for those surviving a loved one's suicide. In an honest, sometimes raw, insightful, and eminently practical way, she covers the emotional, legal, financial, and psychological effects as survivors struggle to make sense of the death and grow beyond it.

Recommended for adults whose spouse, relative, or close friend died by suicide

78. Bolton, Iris. *My Son... My Son: A Guide to Healing After Death, Loss, or Suicide.* Atlanta: Iris Bolton Press, 1983.

This moving and powerful book is still considered the best on child or adolescent suicide. Bolton compassionately and clearly covers the emotional, physical, and psychological devastation, including the denial, the lack of knowledge about suicide, and the despair common to survivors. She helps the family cope and come to a point of resolution and peace.

Recommended highly for any family surviving the suicide of a child

79. Smith, Harold Ivan. *A Long-Shadowed Grief: Suicide and Its Aftermath.* Cowley Publications, 2007.

This compassionate, serious discussion includes managing guilt, dealing with other people, finding spirituality, losing naiveté, and learning to go on.

An excellent resource for anyone who has experienced a death by suicide

80. Rubel, Barbara. *But I Didn't Say Goodbye: For Parents and Professionals Helping Child Suicide Survivors.* GriefCenter, 2000.

This story of a child survivor and the adults in his life helps children deal with the difficulties and the stigmatizing aftermath of suicide. The end of each chapter includes worksheets and exercises that can help both parent and child if they complete them together.

Recommended for parents and other adults helping a child affected by suicide

81. Rubel, Barbara. *But I Didn't Say Goodbye: Helping Children and Families After a Suicide.* 2nd edition. Kendall Park, NJ: Griefwork Center, Inc. 2009.

Barbara Rubel's second book on suicide builds upon her first book and, rather than being aimed at parents and professionals, is more specifically aimed at children and families. As the numbers of suicides increase, including more girls, older adults, and post-traumatic stress disorder (PTSD) veterans, this book's format of a conversational workbook is helpful.

Recommended for family and friends, first responders, clergy, counselors, and anyone affected by suicide

82. Bialosky, Jill. *History of a Suicide: My Sister's Unfinished Life.* Atria, 2011.

Kim was a beautiful, tenderhearted twenty-one-year-old when she took her own life. Her half-sister Jill was heartbroken and haunted by Kim's inexplicable decision. She took nearly twenty years to process the questions, conduct research on suicide in young people, and create this invaluable memoir that combines science, psychology, and the agony of surviving a loved one's suicide. It is honest, riveting, authentic, and eminently useful.

Recommended for family, friends, and loved ones before and/or after a suicide

83. Shneidman, Edwin S. *The Suicidal Mind.* Oxford University Press, 1998.

This classic book remains the best means to understand the underlying processes and thoughts of a suicidal person. It is a somewhat academic book written by the groundbreaking researcher in the area of suicide, but it's accessible to everyone. He describes five clusters into which most suicides fall and ten psychological commonalities among suicides.

Recommended for those who want to undertake a serious investigation of the causes and underlying factors behind suicide

84. Linn-Gust, Michelle & Julie Cerel. *Seeking Hope: Stories of the Suicide Bereaved.* Chellehead Works, 2011.

Every time a person dies by suicide, family and friends are left behind to grieve, regret, wonder, and cope. This is a helpful collection of first-person stories written by loved ones after a suicide. They are honest accounts that illustrate the complicated grief and stigma that follows suicide but also offer hope and healing for survivors.

Recommended for anyone affected by a suicide

Murder or Violence

85. O'Hara, Kathleen. *A Grief Like No Other: Surviving the Violent Death of Someone You Love.* Marlowe and Company, 2006.

The author is a licensed therapist who has counseled hundreds of grieving people. When her own son was brutally murdered, she developed these concrete, practical steps to help guide the family and friends of a murder victim through the complicated vortex of grief that follows violent death.

Recommended for survivors of a murder, victim service providers, and friends

86. Bucholz, Judie A. *Homicide Survivors: Misunderstood Grievers.* Baywood, 2002.

The author is a murder victim survivor who collected stories of families that have faced this terrible tragedy. It follows survivors through court trials and publicity, the emotional roller coaster, and the awkwardness of conversations with others. The book provides a compassionate, honest look at the complicated grief process on personal and social levels.

Recommended for survivors of a murder and those who wish to companion them

87. Lord, Janice Harris. *No Time for Goodbyes: Coping with Sorrow, Anger and Injustice After a Tragic Death.* Bargo, 1991.

Lord, a death educator and grief counselor, has written an invaluable aid to those whose loved ones were murdered, killed by a drunk driver, or died in other violent and tragic circumstances. Lord deals with the possibility of trials, public attention, shock, denial, and all of the intense emotions that swirl through a family struck by sudden, violent death.

Recommended for families dealing with violent death

88. Holmes, Margaret M. *A Terrible Thing Happened: A Story for Children Who Have Witnessed Violence or Trauma.* Magination Press, 2000.

This sensitive book tells the story of Sherman Smith, who saw a terrible thing happen. The "thing" is never named, allowing children to insert their own experience as they walk through Sherman's tale. He tries at first to forget or ignore it, but that makes him feel funny and have bad dreams. He only feels better when he meets someone who helps him talk about the terrible thing.

Recommended for adults who live or work with young children who witness abuse, murder, suicide, an accident, or another traumatic experience

Pet Death

89. Sife, Wallace. *The Loss of a Pet.* 3rd edition. Howell Book House, 2005.

The founder of the Association for Pet Bereavement writes a wide-ranging but concise book detailing the grief a pet owner feels when his or her beloved companion dies or has to be given up due to circumstances beyond anyone's control. He recognizes the special bond older people form with their pets, especially if they're single, and the special attachment of children to animals. He discusses euthanizing pets, including whether to stay with the pet until the last breath, and he covers the stages of pet grief, techniques for dealing with anger, recognizing deeper problems that are masked by mourning, pet cemeteries, and the impact of religious beliefs (with articles by a number of religious leaders). This is the most comprehensive book available for the death or loss of a pet.

Highly recommended for any adult who loves a pet

90. Greene, Lorri A. *Saying Good-Bye to the Pet You Love: A Complete Resource to Help You Heal.* New Harbinger, 2002.

The author is a psychologist recognized for her expertise in pet grief. She writes in practical but compassionate terms about the often-misunderstood feelings people have after the pet they love dies. She discusses the importance of the human-animal bond and offers strategies for working through the grief process.

Recommended for any adult whose pet has died

91. Tuzeo-Jarolmen, JoAnn. *When a Family Pet Dies: A Guide to Dealing with Children's Loss.* Kingsley, 2006.

This is an easy-to-read, comprehensive guide for understanding a child's grief when a beloved family pet dies. The author discusses age-based comprehension, whether or when to get a new pet, and how to address the child's emotional needs in ways that help him or her move on.

Recommended for parents after the death of a family pet

Conclusion

In this book, we face the issues that make most people terribly uncomfortable. We name realities we don't want to face. We teach lessons that are learned best in the crucible of pain.

Why would you choose to read such a book? There is one fundamental reason: Life is an hourglass, and it is stuck to the table. None of us knows how many grains of sand we have left in the top, and none of us can stop the last grain of sand from going through to the bottom. We are not in control, and life can be forever changed in the flash of an instant.

While you still have sand remaining in your hourglass, every single grain is precious. Life is more vibrant when you are aware of the gift in each moment. You take less for granted when you acknowledge that you do not truly "own" anything, for it can all disappear tomorrow. You live with more kindness, tolerance, perspective, and gratitude when you realize you don't know how long you will have the people you love. You help others heal and regain joy when you know how to effectively companion them through the toughest times of life. Awareness of the fragility and tenuous nature of life provides meaning you cannot gain any other way.

At Corgenius, we hope you have the courage to face these difficult topics. We hope you choose to live as fully as possible until you take your last breath and help others to do the same. Use these lessons to make the most of every single grain of sand in the hourglass of your life.

Thank you for spending a few of those precious grains with us.

Keep In Touch

We'd love to hear your stories, questions, and input. Tell us what works best for you or what you learned that made a difference. Tell us what else you'd like to know, so we can include it in the next edition of this book.

You may want to take advantage of our other services as well. Twice a year, Corgenius sponsors a multi-day class of in-depth learning about this material, including role-playing exercises, written work, and table talk. Attendees build a nationwide network to share best practices and hone their skills.

If you prefer private training, Corgenius will come to your office to teach your entire staff.

We also teach client events, making it obvious to clients and prospects that you are a professional who cares about more than just their money. You care about their lives, and you provide unique and valuable information they'd have a hard time getting anywhere else.

E-mail hello@corgenius.com or call us at 847-882-3491. We're committed to doing whatever we can to help you walk your clients through the toughest times of their lives. Dare to make a difference, both personally and professionally.

We look forward to hearing from you.

Bibliography of Resources Used

Anna Nalick's song "Breathe" contains the lyrics "And life's like an hourglass, glued to the table." We are indebted to Anna for that inspiration.

Allianz American Legacies Study: available at https://www.allianzlife. com/MediaCenter/AmericanLegacies.aspx

Alzheimer's Association: available at http://www.alz.org, with many specifics located at http://www.alz.org/downloads/Facts_Figures_2011.pdf

Attig, Thomas. *How We Grieve: Relearning the World.* Oxford University Press, 2011.

Boss, Pauline. *Ambiguous Loss: Learning to Live with Unresolved Grief.* Harvard University Press, 1999.

Bridges, William. *Making Sense of Life's Changes.* Da Capo Press, 2004.

Byock, Ira. *The Four Things That Matter Most: A Book About Living.* Free Press, 2004.

Byock, Ira. *The Best Care Possible: A Physician's Quest to Transform Care Through the End of Life.* Avery, 2012.

Callanan, Maggie & Patricia Kelley. *Final Gifts: Understanding the Special Awareness, Needs, and Communications of the Dying.* Simon & Schuster, 2012.

Center for Disease Control and Prevention. "National Vital Statistics Report 2012." Located at http://www.cdc.gov/nchs/nvss.htm

Chochinov, Harvey M., Linda J. Krisjanson, Thomas F. Hack, Tom Hassard, Susan McClement, & Mike Harlos. "Dignity in the Terminally Ill: Revisited." *Journal of Palliative Medicine.* Vol. 9 No. 3, June 2006. 666–672.

Corr, Charles A. & Donna M. Corr. *Death and Dying, Life and Living.* 7th edition. Wadsworth Publishing, 2012.

DeSpelder, Lynne Ann & Albert Lee Strickland. *The Last Dance: Encountering Death and Dying.* McGraw-Hill, 2008.

Doka, Kenneth J. & Terry L. Martin. *Grieving Beyond Gender: Understanding the Ways Men and Women Mourn.* Taylor & Francis, 2010.

Doka, Kenneth J. *Living with Grief: After Sudden Loss, Suicide, Homicide, Accident, Heart Attack, Stroke.* Taylor & Francis, 1996.

Doka, Kenneth J. *Disenfranchised Grief: Recognizing Hidden Sorrow.* Lexington Books, 1989.

Fagerlin, Angela & Carl E. Schneider. "Enough: The Failure of the Living Will." *Hastings Center Report.* Vol. 34 No. 2, 2004. 30–42. Available online at http://www.thehastingscenter.org/pdf/publications/hcr_mar_apr_2004_enough.pdf

Goldman, Marlene B. & Maureen C. Hatch. *Women & Health.* Academic Press, 2000.

Jordan, John R. & John L. McIntosh. *Grief After Suicide: Understanding the Consequences and Caring for the Survivors.* Routledge, 2010.

Kessler, David. *The Needs of the Dying: A Guide for Bringing Hope, Comfort, and Love to Life's Final Chapter.* Harper Collins, 1997.

Meager, David K. & David E. Balk (eds.). *Handbook of Thanatology: The Essential Body of Knowledge for the Study of Death, Dying, and Bereavement.* Routledge, 2007.

Miller, Mark D. & Charles F. Reynolds III. *Depression and Anxiety in Later Life: What Everyone Needs to Know.* Johns Hopkins Press, 2012.

Mitchell, Kenneth R. & Herbert Anderson. *All Our Losses, All Our Griefs: Resources for Pastoral Care.* Westminster John Knox Press, 1983.

Morris, Virginia. *Talking About Death Won't Kill You.* Workman Publishing, 2001.

Morrison, R. Sean, Ellen Olson, Kristan R. Mertz, & Diane E. Meier. "The Inaccessibility of Advance Directives on Transfer from Ambulatory to Acute Care Settings." *JAMA.* Vol. 274 No. 6, 1995. 478–482.

Neimeyer, Robert A. (ed.) *Meaning Reconstruction and the Experience of Loss.* American Psychological Association, 2001.

Ramirez, Gerardo & Sian L. Beilock. "Writing About Testing Worries Boosts Exam Performance in the Classroom." *Science,* Vol. 331 No. 6014, 2011. 211–213.

Rando, Therese A. (ed.) *Clinical Dimensions of Anticipatory Mourning: Theory and Practice in Working with the Dying, Their Loved Ones, and Their Caregivers.* Research Press, 2000.

Rando, Therese A. *Grief and Mourning: Accommodating to Loss.* In Hannelore Wass & Robert A. Neimeyer (eds.), *Dying: Facing the Facts.* 3rd edition. Taylor and Francis, 1995.

Spencer, Sabina A. and John D. Adams. *Life Changes: A Guide to the Seven Stages of Personal Growth.* Paraview Press, 2002.

Stroebe, Margaret, Henk Schut, & Jan van den Bout (eds.). *Complicated Grief: Scientific Foundations for Health Care Professionals.* Routledge, 2012.

Stroebe, Margaret & Henk Schut. "The Dual Process Model of Coping with Bereavement: Rationale and Description." *Death Studies.* Vol. 23 No. 3, 1999. 197–224.

Werth, James L. & Laura Crow. "End-of-Life Care: An Overview for Professional Counselors." *Journal of Counseling and Development.* Vol. 87 No. 2, 2009. 194–202.

Winokuer, Howard R. & Darcy L. Harris. *Principles and Practice of Grief Counseling.* Springer Publishing, 2012.

Worden, William. *Children and Grief: When a Parent Dies.* The Guilford Press, 2001.

Worden, William. *Grief Counseling and Grief Therapy,* 4th edition. Springer Publishing, 2008.